NORTEÑA

NORTEÑA

AUTHENTIC FAMILY RECIPES FROM THE NORTH OF MEXICO

KARLA ZAZUETA

PAVILION

ESENCIALES DEL NORTE ——

DEL HUERTO ——

DEL MAR ——

DEL RANCHO ——

ALGO PICOSITO

FINAL DULCE ——

PARA LA SED ——

 VEGETARIAN  **VEGAN** 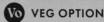 **GLUTEN FREE** **Vo** **VEG OPTION**

INTRODUCTION

One of my first Mexican food memories is eating a *burrito* that my dad had made, sitting in a bus on one of our many journeys to Sinaloa. The smell of the soft homemade flour tortilla, stuffed with a delicious, melt-in-your-mouth shredded beef stew is something that always makes me think of home.

I'm from Ensenada in the north of Mexico, a small coastal city in Baja California – hence the book's title *Norteña*, which means a native woman from northern Mexico, according to the *Collins Dictionary*. It is pronounced nᵊʀ'tenja. My dad was born there and my mum is from Sinaloa, another northern state.

I grew up *Norteña*, stretching out my ch's, talking *golpeado* (abruptly), listening to *Norteñan* and *banda Sinaloense* music. I went to *carne asadas* (north Mexican barbecues), ate flour tortillas, *dogos* (Mexican hot dogs), *nachos* and corn on the cob on the beach while running around with my siblings.

In my house, the outside built-in grill was the heart of the kitchen and we needed no excuse to light it up. Even though I have been living in London for the last twenty years, I still cook the same family recipes that I grew up eating. I'm living proof that you can take a *Norteñan* out of the north, but you can't take the north out of a *Norteña's* heart.

A NORTHERN FAMILY AFFAIR WITH FOOD

Both sides of my family are big and full of excellent cooks. My dad was one of eight: four brothers and four sisters. My mum is one of fourteen: seven sisters and seven brothers. I spent my childhood playing *a la comidita* (pretending to run a restaurant) and hide and seek with my three siblings and my many, many cousins. This was especially true when we used to go to Culiacán, a city in Sinaloa, where my mum is from. I have lovely memories of spending every school holiday at my grandma, Mamá Mila's, house. I will never forget the food she cooked for us, like the *calabaza en dulce*, pumpkin in syrup (page 152). We looked forward to being there so much that we didn't even mind the 24-hour bus journey to get there.

I used to enjoy the summers there as they were full of fun; lots of cousins to play with, fresh *ceviche, raspados* (flavoured shaved ice) and getting wet under the warm rain. However, the heat was – and still is – unbearable. It feels like an inferno on earth. My favourite month to visit my grandma in Sinaloa is December because the climate is far more pleasant during that time of the year. Plus, we loved all the festive gatherings; the feasts and the commotion that the Zazuetas have always made.

December is also the season for making plentiful amounts of *tamales* (page 102) to celebrate Christmas Eve. *Tamales* are dough parcels, stuffed with meat and vegetables, wrapped in corn husks and then steamed. It is a laborious recipe, but I remember the process always being very well-orchestrated by my grandma – the queen of the kitchen and the woman with the best *sazon* (magic touch) in the family. The women of the family would make so many that we would be eating them for days, long after Christmas Eve.

Growing up in a large family meant having a feast at every mealtime. We would have to eat in 'rounds' as there wasn't enough room at the table for everybody to be seated at once. My grandma's house was always crowded like this, with people and food. She and my aunties took the Mexican phrase '*mi casa es tu casa*' (my house is your house) to heart. That way of thinking is embedded in me – because I now do the same.

My mum's family's love for food shaped the way I think about it, but it was my dad's passion for cooking that really instilled in me the desire to learn how to cook. He came from humble beginnings so, out of necessity, learned how to cook from a very young age. He taught my siblings and I all he knew. His happy place was always the kitchen, where he cooked the most amazing food, from traditional Mexican dishes to new things that we had never heard of before.

My apa (dad) was always thinking about food. I was accustomed to listening to him during breakfast, talking about what we were going to eat for lunch. My mum used to tell him off all the time, saying: 'Martin, you are always thinking about food!'. But he never cared about her jests and jeers; food was his love.

My dad was a proper northerner, totally in love with his grill. I remember his eyes lighting up when he got his brick grill built. He made sure to use it as much as he could. I have so many lovely memories of all the *carnes asadas* (barbecues) we had. I can still picture him sitting in a corner of our patio with a wooden chopping board and his knife, chopping the grilled *arrachera* (bavette steak) that he had just taken off the grill. He would put some in a bowl for us to help ourselves to *tacos de carne asada* (page 20). Writing about my dad brings tears to my eyes as we have never been able to recover from his sudden passing. The built-in barbecue has hardly been used since he died, as *carnes asadas* are just not the same without him.

Over the years, the dynamic in my family has changed, especially after the passing of my dad and my grandparents. Now, I live in London and have two children, Miah and Emilio, with my English husband, Russell. I haven't been to Sinaloa in such a long time, but we fly to Ensenada almost every summer. At home in London, I cook a lot of the food that I ate while growing up in Mexico, in the hope that my children come to cherish these recipes as much as I do. I hope they can build their own Mexican food memories and learn that the best way to show someone your love is by cooking, just like my parents did for me.

The list of northern cuisine dishes is so immense that a cookbook is not enough to encapsulate the beautiful flavours of each state. In this book, not only will you find the recipes I grew up with, but also some of the most popular and loved recipes that the north has to offer. Some of the recipes come with useful notes, with what elements can be made ahead of time, how to store the leftovers and what to use to make it vegetarian. Some of the recipes call for easy-to-source alternative ingredients that work well as replacements for traditional Mexican elements – I have cooked all these dishes in my English kitchen.

The recipes are divided into sections: breakfasts, vegetables, seafood, meats, salsas, sweets and drinks. Be sure to use the menu guide to refer to how to serve dishes, when to have them or if they are perfect for a special occasion or a feast.

Here lies a small gathering of northern recipes – each is full of wonderful flavours that offer a great taste of north Mexico.

With love from a very proud *Norteña,*

BUENOS DÍAS

GOOD MORNING

Mexicans love to start their day with a proper, substantial breakfast. A Mexican breakfast always involves eggs, tortillas, beans, spicy salsa, coffee, orange juice, fresh fruit and something sweet to finish with our coffee. It is what keeps us going through the morning, until we sit down for lunch around 3 o'clock.

Mexican breakfast dishes vary depending on the region. For instance, in Yucatán, a typical Mexican dish is *huevos motuleños*, two fried eggs over a fried corn tortilla, covered with a spicy habanero salsa, peas, ham and fried plantain, originally from the city of Motul. In Mexico City, eating *chilaquiles*, fried tortilla chips smothered with a green or red sauce, for breakfast is a must.

Breakfasts in the north of Mexico are just as delicious. In fact, in Valle de Guadalupe, in the countryside of Ensenada, there is a restaurant called La Cocina de Doña Esthela (Doña Esthela's kitchen), which has won the title of being one of the best places in the world to eat breakfast. If you want to eat here, you need to get up very, very early, as the queue for a table is immense – so long that sometimes people wait for up to 3 hours.

A typical northern-style breakfast includes some sort of meat, like steak, *machaca*, chorizo or *barbacoa* (a meat dish traditionally made in an underground oven), eggs, flour or corn tortillas, refried pinto beans, spicy salsa, good coffee and a refreshing orange juice.

In my family, my dad was always up for cooking a feast in the morning, he didn't mind waking up very early to make flour tortillas, fried eggs, refried beans and a salsa from scratch. He used to spoil us all the time, sometimes we'd rise early, hit the road and head towards the countryside to eat at Meson Leonardo's. My dad would always order the same thing, a *querendon*: two fried eggs over a corn tortilla, ranch-style steak, two *quesadillas* and refried pinto beans. It is a wonderful place, extremely popular among the locals, with a wide Mexican breakfast selection.

In this menu plan, you will find light options to start your day, heavy ones to keep you going or the perfect breakfast dish for when you had too many drinks the night before.

MENU 1: A TRADITONAL NORTHERN BREAKFAST

FLOUR TORTILLAS (PAGE 16) Ⓥⓞ
DRIED SHREDDED BEEF WITH POTATOES (PAGE 109)
JUST-FRIED PINTO BEANS (PAGE 45) Ⓥ
CHARRED SALSA (PAGE 138) ⓋⓈ
FRIED EGGS
FRESH FRUIT PLATTER
COFFEE FROM THE POT (PAGE 168)
FRESH ORANGE JUICE
PALMIERS (PAGE 156)

MENU 2: A HANGOVER CURE

CORN TORTILLAS (PAGE 18) ⓋⓈ
SKATE WING SOUP (PAGE 84)
SEAFOOD COCKTAIL (PAGE 86)
FRESH ORANGE JUICE
MICHELADA (PAGE 166)

MENU 3: VEGETARIAN Ⓥ

FLOUR TORTILLAS (PAGE 16) Ⓥⓞ
VEGAN CHORIZO WITH POTATOES (PAGE 44) ⓋⓈ
JUST-FRIED PINTO BEANS (PAGE 45)
CHILLI COLORADO SAUCE (PAGE 32) ⓋⓈ
GUACAMOLE (PAGE 27) ⓋⓈ
FRIED PLANTAIN
COFFEE FROM THE POT (PAGE 168)
A SLICE OF DATE LOAF CAKE (PAGE 149)

MENU 4: SOMETHING SPECIAL

CORN TORTILLAS (PAGE 18) ⓋⓈ
BEEF BIRRIA (PAGE 96)
PIGGY BEANS (PAGE 232)
SCRAMBLED EGGS
COFFEE FROM THE POT (PAGE 168)
PALMIERS (PAGE 156)

ESENCIALES DEL NORTE

NORTHERN ESSENTIALS

It is almost unthinkable to imagine a northern Mexican table without warm, homemade flour tortillas, spicy *salcitas* (salsas), good refried pinto beans or *frijoles puercos* (piggy beans). I'm certain that every north Mexican family holds their own perfect recipe for *carne asada* (charcoal grilled steak), *machaca* (dried shredded beef) and *chile colorado* (red sauce).

These are recipes that are embedded in us, that we grow up with, cook and repeat – sometimes on a daily or weekly basis. Some of the recipes in this section have been passed from generation to generation, like the piggy beans or *chile colorado*.

The first twelve recipes are the perfect dishes to host a *carne asada* (northern Mexican barbecue). I think it's important to learn how to make them, so you, like me, are able to host a proper northern party (page 132). This is sociable, family food, to be shared and enjoyed together.

TORTILLAS DE HARINA

FLOUR TORTILLAS

MAKES APPROX. 16 TORTILLAS

100G PORK LARD (OR
  VEGETABLE SHORTENING),
  CUBED, PLUS EXTRA FOR
  GREASING
500G PLAIN FLOUR, PLUS
  EXTRA FOR DUSTING
1 TBSP TABLE SALT
250ML WARM WATER

Wheat arrived in the north of Mexico with the first Spanish explorers. The indigenous people of the north found a way to use wheat flour by adopting the ingredient into their traditional tortilla recipe, which was usually made with corn. Each state in north Mexico has its own way of making *tortillas* – in Sonora they are famous for their *tortillas sobaqueras*, a very large tortilla that is hand stretched and then cooked over an iron dome heated with wood. In Chihuahua, they add baking powder to the *tortilla* dough, to make it puff easily. In Coahuila, the *tortillas* are a bit thicker.

There are different ways to make a flour *tortilla*; rolling with a rolling pin, stretching by hand or using an electric tortilla press to pre-cook them. This last one is a bit trickier, as electric tortilla presses are hard to come by in the UK. I use a combination of two methods: starting my tortilla by rolling it with the rolling pin and finishing it off stretching by hand. Whichever technique you decide to use, remember that practice makes perfect.

Take the lard out of the fridge 2 hours before making the tortillas, so it is soft enough to work with.

Place the flour in a large bowl. Mix the salt into the flour and then add the lard. Mix well with the tips of your fingers until it feels and looks sandy. Then add the warm water, bit by bit, mixing well until a dough has formed.

Take the dough out of the bowl and start kneading on the worktop. Knead it well for around 15 minutes to activate the gluten in the flour, until the dough looks soft and smooth.

Once the dough bounces back when pressed, place it back into the bowl and cover with a clean, dry tea towel. Leave to rest for 45 minutes.

After 45 minutes, divide the dough into 50g dough balls and place them on a baking tray. Rub a small amount of lard on top, to make sure they don't dry out, before covering with a clean, dry tea towel again. Leave to rest for a further 15 minutes.

After the dough balls have rested, heat a frying pan over a medium–high heat.

Lightly dust your rolling surface and rolling pin with flour. Place a dough ball on the floured surface and, using the rolling pin, roll into a circular shape until 2mm thick and about 25cm wide. Alternatively, start rolling the dough on the worktop and finish by stretching, using the tips of your fingers to make it perfectly round.

Place the tortilla, one at a time, into the dry, hot frying pan and cook for a few seconds on one side. Bubbles will start rising, which is a good sign of when to flip. Cook on the other side until brown spots appear, which should take around 15 seconds.

Once the tortilla has puffed up, quickly and carefully remove from the frying pan and wrap in a clean, dry tea towel to keep warm.

Repeat the process with the remaining dough balls until you have a pile of flour tortillas.

Enjoy the first tortilla with some salted butter and use the rest to make *tacos de carne asada* or *burritos*.

Store the tortillas in a zip-lock bag to keep fresh and prevent from going stale and hard. Flour tortillas can be stored in the fridge for a few days, or kept in the freezer for a few months. To reheat, defrost for about 2 hours before warming in a hot frying pan.

TORTILLAS DE MAÍZ

CORN TORTILLAS

MAKES 19 TORTILLAS

250G MASA HARINA (GMO-FREE
   CORN FLOUR)
450ML WARM WATER

EQUIPMENT
COMAL (FLAT GRIDDLE PAN)/
   NON-STICK FRYING PAN/
   SKILLET)
TORTILLA PRESS
2 PIECES OF THICK PLASTIC
TORTILLERA (TORTILLA BASKET)
   (OPTIONAL)

Corn, for Mexicans, is the golden jewel of our cuisine – we eat it every day in different forms. For me, the tastiest and most versatile way to eat corn is by making corn tortillas; either to wrap food or use as cutlery.

Being totally honest, in Mexico, this is something that you buy fresh from a *tortilleria* (a tortilla shop that produces and sells freshly made tortillas). Here, they nixtamalize the corn and grind the nixtamal (corn kernels that have been cooked in a solution with limestone and water) to make the dough. This goes into a machine that presses the dough into round tortillas, before they are placed on a conveyor belt and cooked at speed. They make *thousands* a day! As a child, I was sent here to buy my family's tortilla batch. I'll never forget the smell of nixtamal in the *tortilleria*; a warm nutty, tangy aroma reminiscent of oats. The *tortillero* would wrap my order either in paper or a towel. Before they did so, I would always pinch a tortilla and borrow the counter's salt shaker, rolling myself a hot, salty one for the journey home.

I didn't learn to make these before I moved to London and eventually grew tired of bringing tortillas back in my suitcase. I taught myself and even learnt how to make my own nixtamal. That, however, is a longer process, so the recipe below uses masa harina, or GMO-free corn flour, which still makes a perfect corn tortilla.

Place the comal or frying pan over a low heat to warm.

Place the nixtamalized corn flour in a bowl and start adding the water, small amounts at a time. Mix well until well combined and there is no dry flour left in the bowl. The dough needs to be moist and just a bit softer than playdough consistency. If you end up adding too much water, add more flour – or if it is too dry, add more water. Once the dough is ready, cover with a dry, clean tea towel to prevent drying out.

This flour does not need to be kneaded as much as wheat flour, as it is gluten free. As soon as the flour turns into a dough, it is ready to start working with. Weigh out a 35g amount and roll slightly smaller than a golf ball.

Open the tortilla press and place one sheet of plastic on the base. Place the corn dough ball in the centre, pressing it slightly so that it sticks in place. Put the other sheet of plastic on top and close the tortilla press, squeezing slightly to form a small tortilla around 4mm thick. Open the press, flip the tortilla and press again until it is around 14cm in diameter and 2mm thick. Make sure that it is equal thickness all around, to cook evenly.

Increase the heat under the pan. Peel off the top piece of plastic. Place the tortilla in the palm of your hand and carefully peel away the other plastic sheet.

Turn the palm of your hand and carefully place the tortilla straight into the hot pan. Cook for 15 seconds over a high heat before flipping. Cook on the other side for around 15 seconds,

then lower the heat and flip one last time until the tortilla starts to puff. When it has ballooned, remove from the heat and wrap in a tea towel to sit in your *tortillera* (tortilla basket) to keep warm. Repeat with the remaining dough to finish the batch.

─────────────

These tortillas can be stored in a zip-lock bag in the fridge for a few days, or in the freezer for a few months. To reheat, defrost on a worktop for around 2 hours before warming in a hot frying pan.

While you can make corn tortillas by hand, a tradition that a lot of women do in Mexico, investing in a good tortilla press is a great option to make the process quick, easy and enjoyable.

TACOS DE CARNE ASADA

ASADA TACOS

Cooking over fire dates back way before the Spaniards arrived in Mexico, but the technique of grilling meat on a pit in the north started with the arrival of Sephardi Jews that settled in Nuevo León. They introduced new breeds of cattle to the north, which flourished. Nowadays, the northern states in Mexico are the main producers of the country's meat.

A good *taco de carne asada* starts with marinating the steaks. There are different ways to do this in every northern state; some people just add salt and pepper, others have a special blend of spices. In my family, and many others in Baja California, we marinate thin pieces of *arrachera* (bavette steak) with slices of orange, shredded onion, garlic salt and lager. Ask your butcher to thinly slice the meat, if possible. The acid of the orange tenderizes the meat as well as adding extra flavour, which makes an amazing *taco de carne asada*.

SERVES 4, MAKES APPROX. 15 TACOS

15 FLOUR OR CORN TORTILLAS (SHOP-BOUGHT OR SEE PAGES 16 AND 18 FOR HOMEMADE)

240G PINTO BEANS FROM THE POT (PAGE 22)

3 PERFECTLY RIPE HASS AVOCADOS, MASHED

150G WHITE ONION, FINELY CHOPPED

150G FRESH CORIANDER, FINELY CHOPPED

SPICY SALSA OF YOUR CHOICE (PAGES 136–145)

3 LIMES, CUT INTO WEDGES

FOR THE MARINADE

1KG BAVETTE STEAK, THINLY SLICED

1 ORANGE, THINLY SLICED

½ WHITE ONION, THINLY SLICED

1 TBSP GARLIC SALT

200ML LAGER

½ TSP GROUND BLACK PEPPER

TO MAKE THE MARINADE
Place a layer of bavette steak in a large dish, then add some orange slices and some onion. Season with garlic salt and black pepper and continue layering with the rest of the meat. Pour the lager over the steaks. Cover and leave in the fridge to marinate for 30 minutes.

TO GRILL THE STEAKS
Rub the grill with half an onion, then light up the barbecue. Once the charcoal is glowing white and red hot in the centre, it's ready to cook on. Spread the coals so they are evenly distributed at the base layer.

Remove the slices of orange and onion from the steak and discard. Grill the thin steaks for a few minutes on each side, until well done. Remove from the heat and chop, keeping the meat in a lidded bowl to keep warm.

Serve with a selection of dishes of your preference; mashed avocado, chopped onion, chopped coriander, slices of lime, spicy salsa (pages 136–145), *frijoles de la olla* (page 22), *frijoles puercos* (page 23), flour and corn tortillas (pages 16 and 18), *quesadillas*, green pepper strips, *chilitos y cebollitas* (page 31), fresh radishes and grilled chorizo.

I always use bavette steak but you could use other cuts, too. My dad used to cook the steaks well done, but feel free to cook the steak the way you like it. To make this recipe vegetarian or vegan, replace the steak for portobello mushrooms, season with salt and pepper and drizzle with olive oil, omitting the orange marinade.

FRIJOLES PINTOS DE LA OLLA

PINTO BEANS FROM THE POT

Ⓥ

In my family, Mondays were the day for cooking beans – always pinto beans, as those are the most popular beans in the north of Mexico. After cooking, we'd store them in the fridge for use throughout the week. Sometimes to make refried beans, or sometimes just to be eaten fresh with some coriander, onion and *queso fresco* – a proper meal in itself.

As a child, helping my mum clean the dried beans was one of the first things I was asked to help with in the kitchen. I still follow this tradition with my children, here in London. They are great helpers, and this is an easy task to get them involved.

Cooking beans from scratch seems like a difficult thing to do, but believe me, this is one of the easiest recipes to make. Once you start cooking beans from scratch, you will never buy ones in a can again. The secret is to soak them for 2 hours and not add salt until they are soft.

SERVES 6

500G DRIED PINTO BEANS
½ ONION, PEELED, WHOLE
3 GARLIC CLOVES, PEELED
2 FRESH BAY LEAVES
5G SEA SALT

TO SERVE
FINELY CHOPPED ONION
CHOPPED FRESH CORIANDER
QUESO FRESCO OR FETA,
    FINELY CRUMBLED
SPICY SALSA OF YOUR CHOICE
    (PAGES 136–145) OR
    CRUSHED CHILTEPINES

Start by sorting out the beans, making sure there are no broken pieces or little stones. Once cleaned, wash under running water.

Add the beans to a large bowl, cover with water and leave to soak for 2 hours.

Discard the water and place the beans in a saucepan or a cast-iron pot. Add 2 litres of cold water, onion, garlic and bay leaves. Bring to the boil and then put the lid on and reduce the heat to low. Simmer for one hour, adding another litre of hot water if needed.

After an hour, check if the beans are tender; if they are, it's time to add the salt. Cook for another 15 minutes over a low heat until the beans are soft.

Serve some pinto beans in a bowl with some bean cooking broth, then add some chopped onion, coriander and crumbled cheese. Add some spicy salsa or crushed chiltepines for a nice kick.

Once cooked, the beans can either be frozen for up to 6 months or kept fresh in the fridge for up to 5 days.

FRIJOLES PUERCOS

PIGGY BEANS

This recipe is from Sinaloa, but there is a similar recipe from Sonora where it is called *frijoles maneados* (mashed beans). In Nuevo León, the recipe pairs with an *adobo* made with different chillies, ferociously called *frijoles con veneno* (beans with poison).

In my family, we cook these every time we're celebrating: a birthday, Christmas, or another special occasion. The bacon and chorizo add so much smoky flavour to the beans that I could eat them by the spoonful. I love the way my mum makes this at home, with the addition of olives. It's a simple joy to bite into something spicy while experiencing savoury creaminess at the same time.

SERVES 4

20ML SUNFLOWER OIL

60G ONION, CHOPPED

1 GARLIC CLOVE, MINCED

100G SMOKED BACON, CHOPPED

100G COOKING CHORIZO, CHOPPED

500G COOKED UNSALTED PINTO BEANS WITH JUICE

20G PICKLED JALAPEÑOS

40G CHIPOTLE IN ADOBO PASTE

50G CHEDDAR CHEESE, GRATED

20 GREEN OLIVES, PITTED

Heat the oil in a saucepan over a medium–low heat, then add the onion and garlic. Fry for 2 minutes, making sure not to burn them.

Add the bacon and fry for around 5 minutes, then add the chorizo and continue frying for another 5 minutes.

When the chorizo and bacon are cooked, incorporate the cooked pinto beans, along with their juice. Add the pickled jalapeños and chipotle in adobo.

Once the beans are hot, remove from the heat and, using a handheld blender, blend until smooth. Stir in the grated Cheddar and olives.

Return to the heat and as soon as the mixture starts bubbling, remove from the heat and serve. Enjoy these beans as a side dish or as a dip alongside some tortilla chips.

You can make this vegetarian by replacing all the pork ingredients for vegan alternatives. My recipe for vegan chorizo (page 44) is perfect for this dish.

MACHACA

DRIED SHREDDED BEEF

Machaca, machacado, carne seca is meat, generally beef, that has been salted, dried under the sun for a few days, then barbecued and pounded in a *molcajete* (pestle and mortar) with garlic. In my opinion, it is one of the recipes that defines the north of Mexico, as this process of preserving meat is a long respected tradition. Natives to the north of Mexico, like the Tarahumaras and Yaquis tribes, used to dry deer meat during the hot and arid months to be consumed all year round.

There are many dishes that can be cooked with *machaca*. In Durango, they make a *caldo de carne seca* (dried meat broth). People in Sonora and Sinaloa cook it with tomato, onion and green pepper – sometimes potato or whisked eggs are added. *Machaca* is usually eaten with flour tortillas and for breakfast, served with fried eggs on the side or scrambled with the egg mix. This way of preserving meat is also used with seafood and fish. In Baja California Sur, they make stingray and fish *machaca* varieties.

My Uncle Ziger, who lives in Sinaloa, makes an amazing *machaca*, and every time I go to Mexico I bring some home. Making *machaca* here in London isn't easy, as the weather does not help with the natural drying process. Instead, I use my oven and have tried and tested the best ways to get the same results and flavour as my uncle. The key is to get very lean beef cut thinly; brisket or beef fillets are great.

MAKES APPROX. 300G

400G LEAN THIN BEEF STEAKS, BRISKET OR FILLET

1 TBSP SEA SALT, FINELY GROUND

2 SMALL GARLIC CLOVES, FINELY CHOPPED

Ask your butcher to thinly slice the beef, otherwise do it at home, using a very sharp knife. Preheat the oven to the lowest setting.

Rub the steaks with the salt until evenly coated. Place the steaks over a cooling rack and place this on top of an oven tray. Place the tray in the oven and leave to dry for 1.5 hours. Flip the steaks from time to time, so the meat dries out evenly on both sides.

Remove the beef steaks from the oven and warm a grill pan on low heat on the hob. Add the steaks to the pan and dry grill for 10 minutes.

For the last time, place the steaks back on the tray and return to the oven for a further 10 minutes. Remove and leave to cool.

Heat some water and slightly rehydrate the steaks for around 3 minutes to make the next pounding step easier.

Pound the steaks in a *molcajete* or use a pestle and mortar, not forgetting to add the garlic. Pound until the consistency resembles shredded beef.

Store in a container and keep in the fridge for up to 5 days or freeze for up to 6 months.

CHILE VERDE CON QUESO

GREEN PEPPER WITH CHEESE

In the north of Mexico, we cook a lot with long green peppers, whose name differs depending on which state you are in. I grew up calling it *chile California* (Californian chilli), but it is also known as *Anaheim*, *magdalena* or *chile verde* (green chilli). It is a mild pepper with a distinctive sweet flavour.

In the UK, it's difficult to find this type of green pepper, but there is a very good Turkish green pepper called 'Yesil Tatli Biber', which is an excellent alternative and can be found in Turkish grocers. In London, I often use Turkish Kasar Peyniri cheese too, which is similar in flavour to one used in northern Mexico.

SERVES 4

3 ANAHEIM OR TURKISH 'YESIL TATLI BIBER' GREEN PEPPERS

1 TSP SUNFLOWER OIL

10G ONION, FINELY CHOPPED

1 GARLIC CLOVE, MINCED

400G KASAR PEYNIRI OR A MIXTURE OF CHEDDAR AND MOZZARELLA CHEESE, CUT INTO CUBES

Char the green peppers, making sure to turn them from time to time to cook evenly. If using a gas hob, this can be done directly over the burner. If using the oven, use the grill setting. Alternatively, char on a hot barbecue.

After 5 minutes of charring, once blackened all over, place the peppers in a plastic zip-lock bag and seal. Leave the peppers to sweat for 10 minutes, before removing to easily peel away their skins, which can be discarded. Remove and discard the seeds, then cut the peppers into strips.

Preheat the oven to 200°C (180°C fan/400°F/Gas 6).

Heat a small ovenproof frying pan or skillet over a medium heat, add the sunflower oil and, once hot, fry the onion and garlic for 1 minute. Add the cheese cubes and place the pan in the oven for around 5 minutes, or until the cheese melts.

Using oven gloves, remove the pan from the oven and add the green pepper strips. Mix well before serving as a side dish to *tacos de carne asada* (page 20).

GUACAMOLE

Vg

A good guacamole is an essential element that brings a good *carne asada taco* together. This incredible salsa is a Mexican staple. Initially the name was first identified as *ahuacamolli,* which is a union of the Nahuatl words *ahuacatl* (avocado) and *molli* (sauce). The avocado had an erotic significance for the Aztecs and women were not allowed to collect them, since the avocado symbolized testicles.

There are different ways to make guacamole; in Sonora, they add charred green pepper strips, while other states add chopped tomatoes – but this recipe is how we make it in my family. My mum doesn't like the taste of raw onion so softens its flavour with lime juice before adding it to the mashed avocados. We always finish our guacamole with a splash of good-quality extra-virgin olive oil.

SERVES 6

5 PERFECTLY RIPE HASS AVOCADOS
1 SMALL ONION
2 LIMES
20G FRESH CORIANDER
1 JALAPEÑO
1 TSP SEA SALT
1 TBSP OLIVE OIL

Open the avocados and scoop out the flesh with a tablespoon. Mash with a potato masher, leaving some texture.

Chop the onion finely, squeeze some lime juice over the top and leave to sit for a few minutes, while you finely chop the coriander and jalapeño.

Add the onion, coriander and jalapeño to the mashed avocados, squeeze over the rest of the lime juice, then add the salt and olive oil. Taste to check the seasoning.

Serve in a bowl with some *totopos* (tortilla chips) on the side.

SALSA BANDERA

TOMATO, ONION & JALAPEÑO SALSA

I grew up calling this dish *salsa bandera* (flag salsa), so-called because the ingredients are the colours of the Mexican flag: red tomatoes, white onions, green coriander and chilli. Interestingly enough, this salsa is also known in other parts of Mexico as *pico de gallo*, as all the ingredients are finely chopped. Whatever you call it, it is a delicious dish that accompanies hot or cold dishes for any occasion.

SERVES 6

4 SMALL ROMA TOMATOES, FINELY DICED

1 SMALL ONION, FINELY DICED

20G FRESH CORIANDER, CHOPPED

1–2 JALAPEÑOS, CHOPPED

1 TSP SEA SALT

1 LIME

Mix together the tomatoes, onion, coriander and jalapeños in a bowl. Season with the salt and add a squeeze of lime juice. Serve next to a delicious guacamole, as part of your *carne asada*.

PEPINOS CON LIMÓN Y CHILE

CUCUMBER WITH LIME & CHILLI

So simple, but so tasty. I make this recipe all the time at home for my children, so they can enjoy it just like I used to when I was their age. The lime and salt slightly pickles the cucumber and keeps it crunchy; adding a bit of chilli powder makes the whole dish super zingy – perfect for snacking or to have on the side as part of your *taco*.

SERVES 4

2 LARGE CUCUMBERS

2 LIMES

½ TSP SEA SALT

½ TSP CHILLI POWDER

Peel the cucumbers and cut them into thin rings. Place them on a platter and squeeze over the lime juice, then add the salt and chilli powder. Let them marinate for 10 minutes and then eat.

CEBOLLA ENCURTIDA

PICKLED RED ONION

This is a delicious recipe that my family loves making every time we have *sopes* (page 118) or *cochinita* (pork pibil). I love the fact that it can be made in advance and keeps in the fridge for around 5 days. Add it to salads, tacos or quesadillas.

To pickle the onions, my mum uses lime juice, as she loves the mellow flavour it gives. This recipe isn't native to the north of Mexico, but it's very common and versatile as an accompaniment; we always have some when we are enjoying a *carne asada*.

SERVES 4

1 RED ONION
TABLE SALT
JUICE OF 4 LIMES
1 TSP DRIED OREGANO

Thinly slice the red onion and place in a bowl, add a teaspoon of salt, mix and set aside for 10 minutes. This will absorb some of the onion moisture.

Rinse the onion with cold water to get rid of excess salt. Then add the lime juice, a pinch of salt and dried oregano. Mix well, leaving to pickle for at least 1 hour and mixing from time to time.

Serve as part of the other toppings for the *carne asada*. The pickled onion can be kept in the fridge for up to 5 days.

CHILITOS Y CEBOLLITAS TOREADOS

CHARRED CHILLIES & SPRING ONIONS IN A SOY & LIME MARINADE

In Baja California, there is a large Chinese community that arrived in the state over three different periods. The first Chinese migration into Mexico was during 1839 to 1842, as people escaped from the Opium War in China. They settled in Baja California, where the majority became farmers. From 1921 to 1930 a larger group of migrants arrived and came to live in Sonora and Sinaloa. The last group arrived between 1931 to 1945. Whilst trying to cross into the United States, many in this group settled in the city of Mexicali, which is why some of our dishes include Chinese ingredients. This recipe uses soy sauce to add saltiness and an umami depth of flavour.

At home, we would use *chiles güeros* – blonde peppers known in English as 'banana peppers' – but this dish can be made with any type of fresh chilli; jalapeños are easier to source. This dish is called *toreados* (to provoke) as the chilli needs to be pressed and rolled to loosen the seeds, making the level of heat feisty like a provoked bullfighter!

Traditionally, the way to eat these is by eating a mouthful of *taco* followed by a bite of raw *toreado* chilli, so that you get a combination of all the spicy, charred flavour in your mouth at once.

SERVES 6

10 JALAPEÑOS, CLEANED AND WITH STEMS REMOVED

10 SPRING ONIONS, CLEANED AND WITH ENDS CUT

SPLASH OF EXTRA-VIRGIN OLIVE OIL (OPTIONAL)

100ML SOY SAUCE

60ML LIME JUICE

Press and roll the jalapeños to loosen the seeds.

Place the chillies and spring onions over a hot barbecue or a dry, hot frying pan to char. Toss them around from time to time to blacken evenly. Add a splash of oil if they stick.

Once charred, place the jalapeños and spring onions on a serving plate.

Mix the soy sauce and lime juice and pour the dressing over the vegetables.

Set aside for 10 minutes to marinate, then serve.

SALSA DE CHILE COLORADO

CHILE COLORADO SAUCE

This sauce is made only in the northern states of Mexico, with a particular chilli from the northern region called *chile colarado*. The name comes from the colour of the chilli; *colorado* meaning 'red'.

Use this sauce as staple to make *enchiladas*, *tamales* or stews with meat and vegetables – like pork, beef, chicken, *nopalitos* (tender cactus), green beans, or potatoes. My dad used to love eating *chile colorado* with pork and *nopalitos*, it was one of his signature dishes.

In London, it is quite difficult to find this particular chilli, so a good alternative is *guajillo* chilli, which is widely available online. This is the recipe for the red sauce, but on page 114 it is used to cook Pork in a Red Chilli Sauce.

SERVES 4

- 8 CHILE COLORADO OR GUAJILLO CHILLIES, CLEANED, DESEEDED AND STEMS REMOVED
- 3 ROMA TOMATOES, HALVED
- 1 ONION, CUT INTO CHUNKS
- 3 GARLIC CLOVES, PEELED
- ½ TSP GROUND CUMIN
- 1 TSP SEA SALT
- 1 TBSP SUNFLOWER OIL

Put the chillies, tomatoes, onion and garlic into a saucepan, then add 300ml water. Bring to the boil, then reduce the heat to cook for 10 minutes.

Remove the chillies and vegetables from the saucepan, reserving the water as stock for later use.

Put the chillies and vegetables into a blender, adding the cumin and salt before blending until smooth. Pass the sauce through a sieve, to remove any unwanted seeds or chilli peel.

Heat the oil in a saucepan over a medium heat and add the sauce. Cook for 5 minutes and then add the reserved water. Cook for a further 5 minutes before turning the heat off.

Store in the fridge for up to 4 days or use straight away as an element to another dish.

SALSA DE CHILTEPIN

CHILTEPIN SPICY SALSA

Chiltepin is a little round red chilli that grows wild, mainly in the state of Sonora. A lot of people know it as the 'red gold of Sonora', because it is the most expensive chilli in Mexico, costing around £100 per kilo. This inflated cost is due to the difficulty in growing on farmland. Its medium–high heat makes it a versatile ingredient. In Sonora, people use a *chiltepinero* (a little pestle and mortar) to crush and add it to broths or soups, but it also goes very well in a salsa. The almost fruity flavour makes this chilli especially unique.

My dad always carried some *chiltepines* in his shirt pocket and my mum would carry the *chiltepinero* in her handbag, wherever they went. It was always on hand to make his food spicier. I have inherited that little pestle and mortar and it is my most precious piece of equipment in my kitchen in London.

Finding *chiltepin* in the UK is almost impossible, but a good alternative is dried bird's eye chillies or *piquín* chillies, which you can find in supermarkets/online. For a more authentic salsa, make this recipe in a *molcajete* (pestle and mortar), but if you don't have one, you can just as well use an electric blender.

SERVES 4

2 PLUM TOMATOES
1 GARLIC CLOVE, PEELED
½ TSP SEA SALT
15 DRIED *CHILTEPIN*, BIRD'S EYE OR PIQUÍN CHILLIES

Warm the tomatoes and garlic in a dry, hot frying pan.

After 5 minutes, remove the garlic clove and pound with the salt in a *molcajete* or a pestle and mortar. Add the *chiltepin* chillies and mash well until they have broken down.

After about 10 minutes, once the tomatoes are charred, remove them from the heat and add to the *molcajete*.

Pound the tomatoes to make a salsa and mix well with the chillies. If the consistency is too thick, add some water to loosen it up.

Serve in the *molcajete* as a side dish.

ÉRASE UNA VEZ ...
ONCE UPON A TIME ...

The history of northern Mexico is full of stories of loss and struggle, but despite this, the one thing it has not lost is its resilience in overcoming adversity. It is a region that has received a lot of people; some trying to conquer it, others looking for a place to live in peace, fleeing slavery or war or trying to cross the border in search of the 'American dream'. Whatever their reason, they have shaped the north into what it is today, a place full of strong people.

THE FIRST SETTLERS

The first settlers in the north of Mexico were nomadic and semi-nomadic groups who survived the extreme temperatures of the desert by hunting and gathering. They learned to dry fresh produce to be able to feed themselves during the seasons when fresh food was in short supply and recipes for *machaca* (dried meat, page 24) are found in each of the nine northern states. According to researcher Leopoldo Valiñas, only a very few ethnic groups that inhabited the land in the sixteenth century have survived to the modern day.

Of all the indigenous groups that lived in the Baja California region, only five groups remain living on ranches in the north: the Cochimí, Paipai, Kumiai, Cucapá and Kiliwa communities.

In Chihuahua, the Rarámuri or Tarahumara (people who run) are the biggest indigenous group, but there are also the Pima, Tepehuán and Guarijío. The Rarámuri use corn to produce a sacred alcoholic drink called *tesgüino* (page 169), which is traditionally drunk during Easter.

The Kikapúes live in Coahuila and they are hunters. The Mascogas community is a small Afro-Mexican group, living in the town of El Nacimiento, who settled there after escaping slavery in the USA.

In Sonora, Sinaloa and Chihuahua, only nine indigenous groups have survived: the Pápagos, Low Pimas, Northern Tepehuanes, Opatas, Guarijíos, Tarahumaras, Yaquis, Mayos and Seris communities. The Yaqui play a big part in local cuisine – every Sonorense knows how to cook *wakabaki huacavaque* (page 123); a beef broth cooked in large quantities for special occasions, such as religious festivities, weddings or funerals.

All these groups, with their thousands of years of history, have enriched their region's gastronomy.

MISSIONS & BLOOD: THE SPANISH CONQUEST OF THE NORTH

When the Spanish arrived in Mexico in 1519, they generally settled in the centre and the south. However, when there was no more land to take, they ventured into the wild desert area of the north, intruding on indigenous groups living under their own laws.

The first Spaniards to explore the north were Álvar Núñez Cabeza de Vaca, Nuño Beltrán de Guzmán and Juan de Oñate, around the 1530s. They confronted the indigenous groups of what are now the states of Sinaloa, Sonora and Tamaulipas in battle. Although these groups put up years of resistance, they were eventually defeated by the Spanish and forced to submit to their laws. Around 85 per cent of the indigenous population died in these battles and of diseases like smallpox, measles, influenza and other viruses spread by the Spaniards.

Around 1572, the Jesuits arrived in the north, followed, years later, by the Franciscans and the Dominicans. From 1683 to 1834, the purpose of these clerics was to evangelize and educate the indigenous groups, teaching them supposedly superior European customs. We can't talk about these missions without mentioning Junípero Serra, the father of the missions in California.

The Jesuits founded these missions with the aim of converting the indigenous tribes to Christianity. The 'missions' were strategically established in the centre of a town, erecting a church, and from there they dominated the indigenous people who lived in the area. In nearby places, the Spanish settled in *rancherias* (ranches), working the land and raising cattle. Others were miners, exploiting the land, and sometimes taking indigenous people prisoner, subjecting them to forced labour in the mines. There are many indications that a high number of indigenous people fled the missions, due to the terrible treatment they received from the clerics and other Spaniards. They were not free, and if they disobeyed, they were whipped.

In the peninsula of Baja California, some of the mission churches are still standing and in use for worship. The mission system was a crucial support for the Spanish domination of the north. Combined with the impact of diseases brought to the new world by the Spanish, this meant by 1800, the number of indigenous people had plummeted to a small fraction of the previous population.

Nowadays, the indigenous groups of the north of Mexico are a minority. Despite being the first settlers, some groups have disappeared completely. Although they have a history traced back several centuries, some prejudiced Mexicans unfairly treat these communities as lower-class, and discriminate against them.

DEL HUERTO

FROM THE GARDEN

Even though the majority of the land in the northern states is desert, it contains hundreds of native plants and cacti, some of which are edible.

During the winter, the desert temperatures drop and growth halts. But, after a good amount of rainfall at the end of the summer, the plants come back to life and the desert is revived to a giant garden. *Chochas,* a white flower of the Palma China plant that blooms around Tamaulipas and Chihuahua, can be foraged for eating and is used raw in salads and stews. The *salicornia,* a green plant that grows near the sea, is also edible and used to garnish local dishes like *ceviche.* Salvia is used in fish and seafood dishes to add a herby, sage flavour. These are only a few of the many edible plants found growing wild in the north.

Both of my parents were vegetable lovers. My dad was a keen gardener and the old house, where we lived for the first 15 years of my life, had a garden full of edible plants and fruit trees. It helped that we lived in Baja California, which has a Mediterranean climate that meant everything seemed to grow well. When our new house was built on the same land, most of our plants had to be removed. We managed to keep a 90-year-old fig tree, a lime tree that gives hundreds of juicy and aromatic limes every year and a *sapote* tree (a tropical Mexican fruit, likened to pumpkin and apricot) that my dad loved.

Some of the recipes in this section are recipes my parents would cook at home time and time again; the cabbage recipe on page 51 is one that we would usually eat on the last days of every month, when money was running low. The cactus salad is not exclusively from the north, but is nostalgic of my childhood memories. *Caldo de queso,* however, is a typical broth from Sonora, and the delicious courgette dish, *colache,* derives from Sinaloa.

I hope these delicious dishes inspire you to cook more vegetarian Mexican recipes at home. Just like my parents did, I'd encourage you to try to and use organic produce where possible; it is good for our planet and good for us.

SOPA FRÍA

PARTY PASTA SALAD

Ⓥ

This delicious and easy to make pasta salad is a party classic and common in the north of Mexico. In Sinaloa, they make this salad to serve with *tamales* (page 102) and piggy beans (page 23).
Try serving on top of corn *tostadas* and you'll have a speedy lunch.

SERVES 6

200G MACARONI

2 LARGE ROASTED RED PEPPERS, STEMS REMOVED, DESEEDED AND FINELY DICED

3 CELERY STICKS, FINELY DICED

140G CAN SWEETCORN, DRAINED

FOR THE DRESSING

300ML DOUBLE CREAM

6 TBSP MAYONNAISE

5 SLICES OF AMERICAN CHEESE

1½ TBSP CHIPOTLE IN ADOBO PASTE

½ TSP SEA SALT

PINCH OF GROUND BLACK PEPPER

Cook the pasta according to the packet instructions, then drain and rinse under cold water to cool. Once cold, place in a large bowl. Mix in the red peppers, celery and can of sweetcorn.

To make the dressing, put all the ingredients in a blender and blend until smooth. Careful not to over-blend, to avoid the double cream becoming butter.

Add the dressing to the pasta and mix well. Leave to rest for 10 minutes before serving, for the flavours to develop.

To make this dish vegan, use vegan cream, cheese and mayonnaise. If you want to add some protein, this salad goes well with diced ham, shredded chicken or canned tuna.

CHILES VERDE RELLENOS

STUFFED LONG GREEN PEPPERS

Ⓥ

Chiles rellenos or 'stuffed peppers' is a dish that is made all around Mexico. People usually use *poblano* peppers, but in the north of Mexico we also make them with famous green peppers that are used in a lot of our dishes.

This wonderful recipe is a crowd-pleaser, and the stuffed pepper can be made in advance if you are cooking multiple dishes for a gathering with friends or family. If you can't find long green peppers, just use green bell peppers instead.

SERVES 4

6 LONG ANAHEIM OR TURKISH 'YESIL TATLI BIBER' GREEN PEPPERS, OR GREEN BELL PEPPERS

150G GRATED MOZZARELLA AND CHEDDAR CHEESE MIX

4 PLUM TOMATOES

¼ ONION, PEELED

1 GARLIC CLOVE, PEELED

1 TSP VEGETABLE OIL

½ TSP SEA SALT

PINCH OF DRIED OREGANO

First char the peppers. Put the peppers on a baking tray and under the grill to char. Make sure to flip them once one side is black. This will take around 3 minutes on each side, so keep an eye on them to avoid over charring.

Once charred and still warm, put them in a plastic zip-lock bag and set aside for 5 minutes. The steam will help to remove the burnt skin easily. Remove the skin. Carefully open them lengthways on one side. Remove the seeds and fill with cheese. Set aside.

To make the tomato sauce, put the tomatoes, onion and garlic in a saucepan and add 450ml water. Bring to the boil and cook for 3 minutes.

Remove all the vegetables and transfer to a blender, adding 120ml of the cooking water. Blend into a smooth sauce and set aside.

Heat the oil in a saucepan over a medium heat. Once hot, pour in the tomato sauce, add the salt and oregano and cook for 3 minutes.

Preheat the oven to 200°C (180°C fan/400°F/Gas 6).

Pour the tomato sauce over an oven-proof serving plate and place the stuffed peppers on top. Bake in the oven for 10 minutes, or just until the cheese has melted.

Serve with some more tomato sauce and white rice with sweetcorn (page 57).

To make this vegan, just replace the cheeses with vegan alternatives. This pairs perfectly with *izquiate* (chia and lime water, page 170).

TAQUITOS DORADOS DE PAPA

POTATO FRIED TAQUITOS

This recipe for fried *taquitos* is very similar to the *sopes* recipe on page 118; the addition of garnish is the way people do it in Sinaloa.

At home, my mum loves making these quite often as they are quick and easy to make, especially if you use shop-bought tortillas. The potato mixture can be made a day in advance as well as the pickled red onion – or why not make this recipe with leftover mashed potato?

MAKES 16

3 LARGE RED POTATOES

25G BUTTER

25ML MILK

1 TSP GARLIC SALT

LITTLE PINCH DRIED OREGANO

16 CORN TORTILLAS (SHOP-BOUGHT OR SEE PAGE 18 FOR HOMEMADE)

350ML SUNFLOWER OIL

16 TOOTHPICKS, TO CLOSE THE TORTILLAS (OPTIONAL)

TO GARNISH

150G SHREDDED ICEBERG LETTUCE

1 LARGE CARROT, PEELED AND GRATED

10 RADISHES, SLICED (OPTIONAL)

PICKLED RED ONION (PAGE 29)

1 PERFECTLY RIPE HASS AVOCADO, CUT INTO THIN SLICES

70ML SOURED CREAM

50G WENSLEYDALE CHEESE, GRATED

SPICY SALSA OF YOUR CHOICE (PAGES 136–145)

Peel and cut the potatoes into 3cm cubes, place them in a large saucepan and cover with water. Bring to the boil and cook for 10–15 minutes until soft. Once soft, drain the water and mash the potatoes, adding the butter, milk, garlic salt and oregano. Set aside.

Heat a frying pan over a medium heat and warm the tortillas slightly, so that they are flexible and don't break when folded.

To fill the tortilla, put 2 tablespoons of mashed potato on one half of the warm tortilla and fold over the other side. To make sure they don't open, you can push a toothpick through the tortilla. Set aside ready to fry.

Once all the tortillas are stuffed, heat the oil in a frying pan over a medium heat until it reaches 180°C (356°F). You can test the oil is hot enough by dropping in a piece of tortilla; if it's ready then it should sizzle and oil bubbles should form.

Using a pair of kitchen tongs, place a few *taquitos* into the oil – as many as you can fit in the pan. Fry for about 1½ minutes on each side until golden brown and crunchy.

When the first batch is fried, place them on kitchen paper to absorb any excess oil. Continue frying the rest and placing them on kitchen paper to drain.

Once all fried, gently open each fried *taquito* and fill them with shredded lettuce, grated carrot, 2 radish slices, pickled red onion and an avocado slice.

To serve, place the *taquitos* on a large platter, pouring over some soured cream and scattering with Wensleydale cheese. Serve with spicy salsa on the side.

For these fried *taquitos* you can also use mashed sweet potato, celeriac or even some mushy peas in place of the red potato. You can mix some cooked shredded chicken or beef into the mashed potato, if you like.

CHORIZO VEGANO CON PAPAS

VEGAN CHORIZO WITH POTATOES

Mexican chorizo is completely different from the Spanish chorizo as it is made using *guajillo* and ancho chillies. It can be either cooked on a barbecue, or the outer skin can be removed and the inside meat is fried in a frying pan combined with other ingredients; like potatoes or beaten eggs. There are different types of Mexican chorizo, but the most popular is fresh cooking chorizo, which, after it's been fried, has an almost minced consistency that melts in your mouth.

In Sinaloa, there is a famous brand that makes a delicious vegan chorizo. It is so famous that now they sell their chorizo in different states. My family has been eating vegan chorizo for years and, to be honest, you can't tell the difference. We love eating it with potatoes or scrambled eggs, perfect for a comforting breakfast, over *sopes* (corn patties) or in a flour tortilla, as a *burrito*.

SERVES 4

2 TBSP SUNFLOWER OIL

1 SMALL ONION, DICED

1 GARLIC CLOVE, MINCED

3 MEDIUM RED POTATOES, PEELED AND CUT INTO 1CM CUBES

150G VEGAN CHORIZO

½ TSP SEA SALT

PINCH OF GROUND BLACK PEPPER

FOR THE VEGAN CHORIZO
MAKES 300G

100G DRIED MINCED SOYA, WASHED AND REHYDRATED

5 GUAJILLO CHILLIES, CLEANED, STEMS AND SEEDS REMOVED

½ TSP GROUND CUMIN

½ TSP DRIED OREGANO

½ TSP DRIED MARJORAM

4 BLACK PEPPERCORNS

1 CLOVE

30ML WHITE WINE VINEGAR

30ML SUNFLOWER OIL

1 TSP SEA SALT

To make the vegan chorizo, first rinse the minced soya several times until the water runs clear. Squeeze out all excess water and set aside.

Place the guajillo chillies in hot water for around 10 minutes to rehydrate and soften. Remove and put the softened guajillos in a blender, reserving the water for later.

Add the spices, vinegar, oil, salt and 60ml of the guajillo water and blend until it is a smooth adobo.

Pass the adobo through a sieve to make sure there are no seeds, then add it to the minced soya and mix very well.

Unless using the chorizo immediately in this dish, store in an airtight plastic bag in the fridge for up to 10 days or freeze for up to 6 months.

Heat the oil in a large frying pan over a medium–low heat and add the onion and garlic. Fry for 2 minutes.

Add the potatoes and mix constantly so the potatoes cook evenly. Reduce the heat so they don't burn and cover with a lid to steam at the same time. Cook for 10 minutes, making sure to mix from time to time. Once the potatoes are soft, add the vegan chorizo and mix. Season with salt and pepper. Cook for a further 3 minutes.

They can be served with some eggs on the side, cooked to your liking or over *sopes* (page 118) or make *burritos*.

This recipe is two-in-one as I include my method for making vegan chorizo, which can be used in other recipes. This is a perfect dish for breakfast and keeps very well in the fridge for around 10 days, or can be frozen for up to 6 months.

FRIJOLES PINTOS FRITOS

JUST-FRIED PINTO BEANS

Fried beans is one of those recipes that every family in Mexico knows how to cook, as it's something that we eat almost daily. Whether as a side or by itself, this is a dish that should always be present on a Mexican table. They are called 'just-fried' beans, because the beans are only fried once. If you fry these beans again the following day, by adding a bit more oil, then they become 'refried' beans.

In the north of Mexico, we love to make refried beans with pinto beans, as they are the most commonly used. To make this recipe from scratch, you can use the Pinto Beans from the Pot recipe on page 22, or alternatively, use good-quality cooked pinto beans in a can.

When my dad used to make refried beans at home, he would fry a corn tortilla in pork lard until it was completely black. Then he'd remove it, add the pinto beans, and season with salt before mashing together. Unlike my dad, I make mine with a bit of onion, garlic and sunflower oil.

SERVES 4

4 TBSP SUNFLOWER OIL

50G ONION, CHOPPED

1 SMALL GARLIC CLOVE, FINELY CHOPPED

400G COOKED PINTO BEANS OR A CAN OF COOKED PINTO BEANS, RESERVING THE BEAN JUICE

½ TSP SEA SALT

50G QUESO FRESCO OR FETA CHEESE, CRUMBLED

In a small saucepan, heat the oil over a medium–low heat for a minute or so. Add the onion and garlic and fry for 2 minutes, until the onion is translucent.

Pour in the cooked pinto beans, including the water that they were cooked in. Season with salt and mix well. Bring to the boil and lower the heat, covering with a lid and cooking for 3 minutes.

Turn off the heat and mash with a potato masher or blend with a handheld blender to achieve a smoother, runny consistency.

Place on a platter and serve with some crumbled *queso fresco* as a side dish, or eat with corn tortillas or *totopos* (tortilla chips).

Don't use olive oil to make fried beans – use a flavourless oil instead that lets the flavour of the beans shine. If the beans look to dry, add some bean juice to loosen them up.

ENTOMATADAS DE QUESO

TOMATO ENCHILADAS WITH CHEESE

These delicious *entomatadas* are the cousin of *enchiladas*. As its name suggests, they are made with a tomato purée, so they are super simple. There are many recipes for *entomatadas*, but this is the way my mum makes them. She loves to cut corners when she is cooking, so instead of making the tomato sauce from scratch, she uses tomato purée or passata.

They are a perfect alternative to a spicy *enchilada* as these milder cousins are made without chillies. You can fill them with *queso fresco* or refried beans, I filled mine with ricotta, which is easier to source in British supermarkets.

FOR THE TOMATO SAUCE

125ML PASSATA

½ TSP SEA SALT

PINCH OF DRIED OREGANO

FOR THE ENTOMATADAS

125G *QUESO FRESCO* OR RICOTTA

50G FRESH CORIANDER, CHOPPED

½ TSP SEA SALT

60ML SUNFLOWER OIL

12 CORN TORTILLAS, COLD, (SHOP-BOUGHT OR SEE PAGE 18 FOR HOMEMADE)

TO GARNISH

2 HANDFULS OF THINLY SHREDDED ICEBERG LETTUCE

1 PERFECTLY RIPE HASS AVOCADO, THINLY SLICED

75G *QUESO FRESCO* OR FETA CHEESE, CRUMBLED

60ML SOURED CREAM

Start by making the tomto sauce. Pour the passata into a small frying pan. Add the salt and oregano and bring to a quick boil over a medium heat. Once it starts boiling, turn off the heat and set aside.

Next, make the filling for the entimatadas by placing the *queso fresco* or ricotta in a bowl. Add the coriander and salt, then mix well and set aside.

To construct the *entomatadas*, first gather the tortillas, the cheese filling, warmed tomato sauce and a large plate.

Heat the oil over a medium heat for around 3 minutes, using a clean frying pan, big enough to fry the corn tortillas individually.

Using a pair of kitchen tongs, grab a cold tortilla, fry for one minute, flipping sides halfway through cooking. Grab with the pair of tongs and place in the tomato sauce. Drench the tortilla in it and then remove.

Put on the plate, add 1 tablespoon of the cheese filling then roll the tortilla. Transfer to a platter dish.

Repeat the process with the remaining tortillas until all the *entomatadas* are made and sitting on your platter.

To serve, simply scatter some shredded lettuce, avocado slices, *queso fresco* or feta and soured cream over your platter, to garnish. Serve with some fried pinto beans on the side.

CALDO DE QUESO

CHEESE BROTH

Ⓥ

A perfect broth for a rainy day or … just because! This delicious cheese broth is a favourite of mine, to be eaten when it's cold outside. The traditional recipe is made with green Anaheim chillies and *asadero* cheese (roasting cheese) but using Turkish green peppers, or even green bell peppers, is a great alternative. For the cheese, a reduced-salt halloumi does the job — or, a hard cheese that keeps its shape in the hot broth is even better.

SERVES 4

4 ANAHEIM OR TURKISH 'YESIL TATLI BIBER' GREEN PEPPERS, OR GREEN BELL PEPPERS

1 TBSP SUNFLOWER OIL

½ ONION, FINELY CHOPPED

2 GARLIC CLOVES, MINCED

4 PLUM TOMATOES, GRATED

½ TSP TOMATO PURÉE

BOILING WATER

1 TBSP SEA SALT

4 RED POTATOES, PEELED AND CUBED

400G REDUCED-SALT HALLOUMI CHEESE, CUT INTO 2CM CUBES

100ML WHOLE MILK

Start by charring the green peppers. Place them directly over a gas hob or under the grill, on medium heat, turning them from time to time to char evenly. This will take around 5 minutes. Once they are charred, place them in a plastic zip-lock bag for 10 minutes to sweat; this will help to remove the burnt skin easily.

Remove the chillies from the bag and peel off all the blackened bits and discard. Remove the seeds and stems and cut into thin strips. Set aside.

Heat the oil in a large saucepan over a medium heat, then add the onion and fry for 2 minutes until soft and translucent. Add the garlic and sauté for a minute or so. Add the grated tomato and tomato purée and fry for a further 3 minutes.

Pour in 1.25l of boiling water and season with the salt. Once the broth starts boiling, add the potatoes, before reducing the heat and simmering with the lid on for around 10 minutes until the potatoes are soft.

Add the green pepper and cook for further 3 minutes. Just before turning the heat off, add the cheese and milk and cook for 2 minutes more.

Serve and enjoy by itself or with some rolled-up corn tortillas.

CALABACITAS CON ELOTE

COURGETTES WITH SWEETCORN

This is a great meal for a busy weekday, as this recipe is super easy and fast to make. In Mexico, we usually use white courgettes but, here in London, I love playing around with different varieties, especially when they are in season. This is my go-to recipe for when I don't want to eat meat and am feeling nostalgic for Mexico.

SERVES 4

20G BUTTER

1 TBSP SUNFLOWER OIL

90G ONION, FINELY DICED

1 GARLIC CLOVE, MINCED

3 PLUM TOMATOES, FINELY DICED

750G OR 4 COURGETTES, CUT INTO 2CM DICE

70G FROZEN SWEETCORN

½ TSP SEA SALT

120G *QUESO FRESCO* OR MANOURI CHEESE, CUBED

In a large saucepan, melt the butter and oil over a medium heat. Add the onion and garlic and fry for 2 minutes.

Add the tomatoes, courgettes, sweetcorn and salt. Cover with a lid, reduce the heat and simmer for 10 minutes, or until the courgettes are cooked. Make sure to mix from time to time.

Turn the heat off and scatter the cheese on top. Cover with a lid again and leave for 5 minutes for the cheese to set.

Serve with some red rice and warm corn tortillas (pages 56 and 18).

COLACHE

COURGETTES WITH CHEESE

Colache is a courgette dish popular in Sonora and Sinaloa. There are different version; some without cheese and others that use more sugar than salt. Whichever way it is cooked, the recipe is easy and delicious as a side dish. It can be eaten with warm corn tortillas, over corn *tostadas* or with some rice on the side. Perfect for a quick lunch!

SERVES 4

2 TBSP SUNFLOWER OIL

3 SMALL GREEN COURGETTES, SUPER FINELY CHOPPED

1 TSP SEA SALT

½ TSP CASTER SUGAR

3 TBSP DOUBLE CREAM

200G BUFFALOMI CHEESE OR HALLOUMI

50G MIXED GRATED CHEDDAR AND MOZZARELLA CHEESE

In a frying pan with a lid, heat the oil over a medium heat and add the courgettes. Season with the salt and sugar. Mix well and cook for 10 minutes until the courgettes are soft and pale in colour.

Add the double cream and cook for 2 minutes. When the cream starts bubbling, add the buffalomi cheese, reduce the heat and cover with the lid. Let the cheese cook for a further 3 minutes until it is soft.

Add the grated mix of Cheddar and mozzarella and cover with a lid, to allow the cheese to melt.

Serve with some corn tortillas, *tostadas* or rice on the side.

REPOLLO NORTEÑO

NORTHERN-STYLE WHITE CABBAGE

Ⓥ

It is amazing how your imagination works when you are short of money. This is the dish my parents used to make at the end of the month, when funds were running low.

The crushed *chiltepin* chillies are a distinctly northern addition to this delicious recipe, which might vary in other Mexican regions. You can add some crushed bird's eye chillies or any supermarket brand chilli flakes, as I know it is difficult to find *chiltepin* chilli in the UK. Serve this either as a single side plate or as a main dish, with some rolled up corn tortillas (page 18) and red rice (page 56) on the side.

SERVES 4

20G SALTED BUTTER

2 TBSP SUNFLOWER OIL

3 PLUM TOMATOES, CHOPPED

1 SMALL ONION, CHOPPED

1 SWEETHEART CABBAGE, SHREDDED

½ TSP SEA SALT

120G FROZEN SWEETCORN

3 DRIED *CHILTEPINES* OR BIRD'S EYE CHILLIES, CRUSHED (OPTIONAL)

50G *QUESO FRESCO* OR FETA, CRUMBLED (OPTIONAL)

Heat the butter and oil in a large saucepan over a medium heat. Add the tomatoes and onion and fry for 3 minutes, until the tomato is soft and the onion translucent.

Add the shredded cabbage, 100ml water, salt and sweetcorn, mix well and cover with a lid. Reduce the heat and cook for 10 minutes, mixing from time to time to cook the cabbage evenly.

Once the cabbage turns translucent, remove from the heat and serve on a platter as a main dish with some red rice. To finish the dish, scatter some cheese and crushed chillies on top, if you like.

NOPALITOS A LA MEXICANA

MEXICAN CACTUS SALAD

Cacti grow wild all over Mexico and there are many varieties, but there is a particular *nopal* type that we use for cooking; the *opuntia* variety. There are farms that grow *nopales* and supply markets and supermarkets all around the country. This cactus is a staple and considered a superfood, as it is very nutritious, high in vitamins A, B and C – it even helps controls diabetes and high cholesterol. As well as corn and beans, every Mexican grows up eating *nopales,* and there are a lot of *nopal* recipes.

At home we had a *nopalera,* a little area in our garden that grew *nopales.* My dad used to look after them as if they were another one of his children, and he would cut the young paddles of the *nopal* and clean them with care. This meant getting rid of the spines, before dicing them and cooking in water. He would make wonderful dishes with them, like *nopalitos* with pork, *chile colorado, nopalitos* stew, eggs with *nopales;* but his favourite recipe was this delicious salad, which is probably the best way to serve them.

They are quite difficult to find fresh outside of Mexico, but there are some Mexican food brands that sell them in brine, which is a good alternative. If you get the opportunity to buy them fresh, they are so delicious.

SERVES 4

460G JAR COOKED CACTUS STRIPS

2 PLUM TOMATOES, SMALL DICED

½ ONION, FINELY CHOPPED

8G FRESH CORIANDER, FINELY CHOPPED

1 TBSP VIRGIN OLIVE OIL

½ TSP DRIED OREGANO

¼ TSP SEA SALT

50G *QUESO FRESCO* OR FETA, FINELY CRUMBLED

Open the jar and drain away the brine. Rinse the *nopalitos* strips very well until the salty flavour has gone. Cut into small cubes and place in a salad bowl.

Add the remaining ingredients and mix very well. Set aside for 10 minutes before eating. This will enhance the flavour.

Serve as a light lunch or side dish.

ENSALADA DE BERROS

WATERCRESS SALAD

Ⓥ

My dad loved taking us to the countryside. We would get up early, my parents would make some kind of packed lunch (like a tuna salad or some sandwiches) and off we went! He would park the car just on the side of a brook and we would spend the day there, playing in the water, running around, exploring and eating.

My dad used to go for walks to find 'delicious things', which really was his own words for foraging. He always came back with something and often this was watercress. This recipe is a super easy, fresh salad for a summer's day.

SERVES 4

100G WATERCRESS, WASHED

2 PLUM TOMATOES, DICED

½ CUCUMBER, PEELED AND DICED

80G PICKLED RED ONION (PAGE 29)

7 RADISHES, SLICED

100G *QUESO FRESCO*, FETA OR MANOURI, CUT INTO CUBES

80ML CORIANDER DRESSING (PAGE 145)

Place the watercress in a salad bowl and add the tomatoes, cucumber, pickled red onion, radishes and cheese. Mix well, then add the coriander dressing before mixing again.

Serve immediately.

ENSALADA CAESAR

CAESAR SALAD

Tijuana, a border city in Baja California, is the home of this delicious salad that is now internationally acclaimed. There are many recipe variations for how to make the dressing; I never add chicken, like some recipes do, as this is not traditional. The original Caesar Salad was created in the restaurant of Hotel Caesar, in the 1920s. If you ever have the chance to visit Baja, this place is a must-see stop.

Traditionally, the dressing is made in a large wooden salad bowl and mixed with two wooden spoons, but I start making mine with a handheld blender and finish mixing it by hand – to avoid thickening it too much. I like the simplicity of this salad and enjoying it as it should be, without chicken, but with some croutons.

SERVES 4

½ BAGUETTE

1 TBSP EXTRA-VIRGIN OLIVE OIL

1 ROMAINE LETTUCE WASHED, DRIED AND LEAVES SEPARATED

FOR THE DRESSING

3 ANCHOVY FILLETS, IN OLIVE OIL

1 TSP DIJON MUSTARD

1 SMALL GARLIC CLOVE, MINCED

1 TSP WORCESTERSHIRE SAUCE

1 EGG YOLK

PINCH OF GROUND BLACK PEPPER

JUICE OF ½ LIME

120ML EXTRA-VIRGIN OLIVE OIL

30G PARMESAN, GRATED

To make the croutons, preheat the oven to 200°C (180°C fan/400°F/Gas 6). Tear the baguette into small pieces. Place them onto a baking tray and toss in the oil. Bake for 15 minutes until they are golden brown. Remove from the oven and set aside.

The dressing can be made using a handheld blender to obtain a smooth consistency. Place the anchovies, mustard, garlic, Worcestershire sauce, egg yolk, black pepper and lime juice in a jar and blend. Alternatively, if the anchovy paste is smooth, this step can be done straight into the bowl where the dressing is going to be made.

Once these ingredients are combined, place them into a large salad bowl, preferably a shallow one. Then start slowly pouring in the extra-virgin olive oil, whisking vigorously to emulsify the dressing. The dressing needs to be a thick, pourable consistency.

Once the dressing is ready, add half of the Parmesan and combine. Set aside.

To make the salad, add the lettuce leaves to the bowl and coat them evenly with the dressing. Add the croutons and remaining Parmesan. Toss everything well and serve.

ARROZ MEXICANO
FOUR WAYS FOR MEXICAN RICE

Rice is not a grain indigenous to Mexico but was brought to our country by the Spanish. It received such a warm welcome into our gastronomy that nowadays we can hardly think of a popular Mexican dish without it; *mole poblano* (a Mexican sauce made with chillies, spices, nuts and chocolate from the state of Puebla) and tomato rice, a good fried fish with white rice, or a delicious Mexican rice pudding.

The most common type of rice used for cooking in Mexico is long-grain, but here in London I always use basmati, as it's easier to find. It is light, fluffy when it is cooked and it has a unique nutty flavour. Basmati has become the perfect pairing for a lot of our favourite Mexican dishes.

The spring rice and white rice with sweetcorn are the perfect accompaniments to seafood or fish, whilst the coriander rice on page 57 is delicious paired with vegetarian dishes, like cabbage or courgettes. The best way to serve the red rice (page 56) is with meat dishes like *picadillo* (page 130), chicken, *chile colorado* (Anaheim red chilli sauce) or any other dish with deep flavours. I love eating any leftover red rice with some sliced banana on top or mixed with scrambled eggs for breakfast.

ARROZ PRIMAVERA
SPRING RICE

SERVES 4

160G BASMATI RICE OR LONG-GRAIN RICE

2 TBSP VEGETABLE OIL

½ SMALL ONION, FINELY CHOPPED

1 SMALL GARLIC CLOVE, CHOPPED

1 TBSP SEA SALT

450ML HOT UNSALTED VEGETABLE STOCK

1 SMALL CARROT, PEELED AND DICED

60G FROZEN SWEETCORN

60G FROZEN PEAS

Wash the rice several times until the water runs clear.

In a large saucepan, heat the oil over a medium–low heat. Add the onion and the garlic and fry for 1 minute. Then add the rice and fry for a further minute to coat all the rice grains with the oil, making sure not to burn the rice. Add the salt and mix well.

Reduce the heat and slowly add the vegetable stock, followed by the vegetables. Stir gently, just once, then put the lid on and simmer for around 15 minutes.

Turn the heat off and leave to rest for 5 minutes, then, using a fork, gently mix to separate the grains of rice. Serve on a platter.

ARROZ ROJO

RED RICE

SERVES 4

160G BASMATI RICE OR LONG-GRAIN RICE
3 TBSP VEGETABLE OIL
½ SMALL ONION, FINELY CHOPPED
1 SMALL GARLIC CLOVE, PEELED

2 TBSP TOMATO PURÉE
1 TBSP SEA SALT
450ML BOILING WATER
5 SPRIGS OF FRESH CORIANDER

Wash the rice several times until the water runs clear.

In a large saucepan, heat the oil over a medium heat and add the onion and the garlic and fry for 2 minutes.

Add the rice and fry for a further minute, to coat all the rice grains with the oil.

Add the tomato purée and the salt and fry for 1 minute, stirring continuously to avoid burning. Reduce the heat to very low and add the hot water slowly. Gently mix, add the coriander springs and cover with a lid. Simmer over a low heat for 10–15 minutes, or until the water has evaporated and the rice is cooked.

Turn the heat off and let it rest for 5 minutes before serving. Remove the garlic clove and the coriander sprigs. Separate the grains of rice by fluffing with a fork. Serve either on a big platter or individually next to a portion of a main dish.

ARROZ VERDE

GREEN RICE

SERVES 4

160G BASMATI RICE OR LONG-GRAIN RICE
16G FRESH CORIANDER, STALKS AND LEAVES, PLUS 5 SPRIGS AND EXTRA, CHOPPED, TO GARNISH

450ML BOILING WATER
3 TBSP VEGETABLE OIL
½ SMALL ONION, FINELY CHOPPED
1 SMALL GARLIC CLOVE, CRUSHED
1 TBSP SEA SALT

Wash the rice several times until the water runs clear.

Add the coriander stalks and leaves to half the hot water. Use a handblender to blend until smooth. Add this to the remaining water. Set aside.

In a large saucepan, heat the oil over a medium–low heat, add the onion and garlic and fry for 2 minutes. Add the rice and fry for 2 minutes, mixing continuously to avoid burning.

Season with the salt. Reduce the heat and add the coriander water slowly. Gently mix, add the coriander sprigs and cover with a lid. Simmer over low heat for 10–15 minutes, or until the water has evaporated and the rice is cooked.

Turn the heat off and let it rest for 5 minutes before serving. Remove the coriander sprigs. Separate the grains of rice by fluffing with a fork and serve on a platter. Scatter over some fresh coriander before serving.

ARROZ BLANCO CON ELOTE

WHITE RICE WITH SWEETCORN

Ⓥ

SERVES 4

160G BASMATI RICE OR
   LONG-GRAIN RICE
30G BUTTER
50G CHOPPED ONION

1 GARLIC CLOVE, CHOPPED
½ TSP SEA SALT
450ML HOT VEGETABLE STOCK
120G FROZEN SWEETCORN

Wash the rice several times until the water runs clear.

In a large saucepan, melt the butter over a medium heat and add the onion and garlic. Fry for 2 minutes, then add the rice and fry for 3 minutes, mixing constantly to avoid burning.

Add the salt and continue stirring.

Reduce the heat and add the stock. Then add the frozen sweetcorn, mixing slightly to combine with the rice. Cover with a lid and simmer for 15 minutes until the water has evaporated and the rice is cooked.

Turn the heat off and set aside to rest for 5 minutes, then separate the grains of rice by fluffing with a fork and serve.

NORTEÑOS:
THE PEOPLE OF THE DESERT

The north is vast and composed of nine different states: Baja California, Baja California Sur, Chihuahua, Coahuila, Durango, Nuevo León, Sinaloa, Sonora and Tamaulipas. Each state has their own distinctive way of life.

However, there are two things that they all share – the love of a good carne asada and the desert. The people from the north are strong and brave, and I guess after putting up with the extreme weather and the arid terrain that the desert provides, we are a bit untamed. We never complain about the high heat; we embrace it and have learned to live with it. We wear cowboy hats for shade and boots to protect our feet from the dusty, natural landscape.

The powerful sun has shaped us; it has weathered our skin and given us a squint that looks like we are always in a mood – but we are not! We are the people of the desert: focused, hardworking and very disciplined. We speak loudly, abruptly and frankly, but we have good manners and say hello to everyone who crosses our path. We speak with a strong accent, using anglicisms, because of our proximity with the United States, like la troca (pick-up truck), cachar (to catch) and dar un roll (go for a ride). We call someone's name using the article 'the' first – such as la Karla, el Pedro.

We tend to make friends wherever we go because of our intrinsic ability to organize good gatherings and armar el party (throw a party). We believe that everything can be fixed with a good carne asada (northern Mexican barbecue) and some cheves (beers), which is what we drink when the heat is unbearable. We are happy eating simply; just flour tortillas, machaca (dried meat), seafood tacos and dogos. We play baseball, basketball and American football.

The desert is in us, it is what makes us Norteños. We are very much at its mercy; sometimes it is harsh with us, but even so, we still love it because it has made us strong, has given us a lot, has shaped us and made us who we are, yes, we are the people of the desert and with its unique landscape, we feel proud of calling it our home.

DEL MAR

FROM THE SEA

A vast part of the north of Mexico is surrounded by sea. The Pacific Ocean and the Sea of Cortez lie on the west and the Gulf of Mexico lies on the East. These stretches are rich in seafood and fish, and you can find some astonishing dishes, like fresh seafood cocktails, octopus and oysters.

Ensenada, my hometown, is famous for its fresh seafood. There are a lot of street vendors that sell incredible seafood served from a *carreta* (cart). It's something I recommend experiencing, at least once in your lifetime. Most people have tried the famous Baja fish taco before, or a good *ceviche* or a great seafood cocktail, but having these in the place where they were created is a mind-blowing experience.

There are two carts in particular that we love visiting when we go back: La Guerrerense and El Güero, both based in the tourist area of Ensenada, both run by family members and both serve incredible and super-fresh seafood. Every time we go, we know there will be a long queue for these two popular food carts. However, my husband says I am a proper *Ensenadense* (a person from Ensenada) because, somehow, I manage to defeat the crowds and get served quickly.

My favourite thing to order are *almejas chocolatas*, which are delicious, big, meaty clams — brown in colour (hence their name) and native to this region. You should order an *almeja preparada* (prepared clam), which has a lot of fresh vegetables and lime juice. It's a very simple dish but packed with amazing flavours.

The recipes in this chapter are only a small compilation of all my favourite seafood dishes that I love eating when we go back to the north in the summer to visit my mum.

TACOS DE PESCADO

BAJA FISH TACOS

I'm very proud to say that these tacos are 100 per cent native to Ensenada, even though everyone knows them as Baja tacos. This very famous recipe was reportedly created by Don Mario in the 1960s, in a *taqueria* at Mercado Negro, the city's fish market. He used to sell fried fish in the Bachigualato quarter of Sinaloa, and the fishermen started to ask him to serve the fish in tortillas. That is how the fish taco was born!

The original recipe was made with pieces of angel shark fish, although nowadays it can be fried and served as a taco with any white meaty fish. Later on, another *taquero*, Zeferino Mancilla Fortuna, added the batter to the fish, not knowing that this would make these tacos world famous.

Originally, the fish was fried in pork lard and served over an 18cm corn tortilla. In Ensenada, the recipe changes from taqueria to taqueria and from family to family – this is our way.

MAKES 12–15

12–15 WARM 18CM DIAMETER CORN TORTILLAS (SHOP-BOUGHT OR SEE PAGE 18 FOR HOMEMADE)

2 LIMES

SPICY SALSA OF YOUR CHOICE (PAGES 136–145)

SALSA BANDERA (PAGE 28)

PICKLED RED ONION (PAGE 29)

3 HANDFULS OF ICEBERG LETTUCE, FINELY SHREDDED

FOR THE FISH PREP

140G SELF-RAISING FLOUR (OR PLAIN FLOUR WITH 1 TSP BAKING POWDER ADDED)

1 TSP SEA SALT

½ TSP DRIED OREGANO

1½ TBSP AMERICAN MUSTARD

⅛ TSP GROUND BLACK PEPPER

200ML LAGER

300G FRESH SKINLESS AND BONELESS COD LOIN

3 TBSP PLAIN FLOUR, FOR COATING

450ML VEGETABLE OIL

FOR THE MAYONNAISE

60ML SOURED CREAM

60ML MAYONNAISE

2 TBSP MILK

PINCH OF SEA SALT

PINCH OF GROUND BLACK PEPPER

To make a batter for the fish, combine the flour, salt, oregano, American mustard, black pepper and lager in a mixing bowl. Set aside.

Cut the fish fillet into thin 5cm x 3cm pieces. Pat the pieces of fish dry with kitchen paper to remove any moisture. Place the plain flour on a plate and flour the fish, making sure to remove any excess flour. Add the pieces of fish to the batter and place in the fridge until ready to fry. This step can be done a few hours in advance to save time.

In a small bowl, mix the mayonnaise, soured cream, milk, salt and pepper together. Set aside.

Heat the tortillas and wrap them in a tea towel to keep warm. Cut the limes into wedges and put the spicy salsa in a bowl.

Heat the oil in a deep saucepan until it reaches 190°C (374°F) on a cooking thermometer. If you don't have one, check if the oil is ready by dropping some batter into the oil. If it turns brown in 15 seconds, it is ready.

Take a piece of fish from the batter, removing any dripping excess, then place into the oil and fry for 2 minutes on each side, flipping using kitchen tongs. When the fish is golden brown and crispy, remove the pieces and drain on some kitchen paper.

Take a tortilla, spread with some mayonnaise mixture, add two pieces of fried fish, some shredded lettuce, salsa bandera, pickled onion and spicy salsa. Finish with a squeeze of lime juice.

These tacos can be made using prawns or even steamed cauliflower florets for a vegetarian option.

TACOS GOBERNADOR

PRAWN & CHEESE TACOS

If you want a prawn taco recipe up your sleeve, this is the one you need. The recipe for these tacos comes from Mazatlán, Sinaloa. The story goes that the owner of Los Arcos restaurant, Francisco Labastida, came up with this idea to impress the governor, who was visiting. That is why he called them governor tacos!

MAKES 12

1 TBSP VEGETABLE OIL

15G SALTED BUTTER

½ ONION, FINELY DICED

1 GARLIC CLOVE, FINELY CHOPPED

1 CELERY STICK, FINELY DICED

1 *POBLANO* OR GREEN PEPPER, CHARRED, DESEEDED AND CHOPPED

1 TOMATO, FINELY DICED

400G PRAWNS, PEELED, CLEANED AND CHOPPED

1 TSP SEA SALT

PINCH OF GROUND BLACK PEPPER

JUICE OF ½ LIME

TO SERVE

12 CORN TORTILLAS (SHOP-BOUGHT OR SEE PAGE 18 FOR HOMEMADE)

500G MIXED GRATED MOZZARELLA AND CHEDDAR CHEESE

In a large frying pan, heat the oil and butter over a low–medium heat. Once the butter has melted, add the onion and garlic and fry for 3 minutes until translucent.

Add the celery and *poblano*. Continue frying for 3 minutes, mixing from time to time to avoid burning. Add the chopped tomato and cook for a further 3 minutes.

Once the vegetables are fried, add the prawns. Season with the salt and pepper and cook for 10 minutes on a low–medium heat until the prawns are pink and properly cooked. Squeeze over the lime juice and set aside while you heat the tortillas.

Heat each tortilla in a pan over a medium heat, adding some cheese and letting it melt. Top with some of the prawn stew and serve.

You can use florets of roasted cauliflower instead of prawns for a vegetarian option.

CEVICHE DE CAMARÓN

PRAWN CEVICHE TOSTADAS

This tasty and refreshing dish is usually made with minced or finely diced fish or seafood. It is 'cooked' by the acidity of lime juice and served straight away. Everyone in Mexico knows that the best *ceviche* is found in places near the coast, as it's almost certain that you will get very fresh fish or seafood. In Sinaloa, they also add diced cucumber, Clamato juice and Maggi sauce.

Ensenada, my hometown, is one of the most famous port cities in Mexico for its amazing seafood and fish, so, we make *ceviche* a lot. At home in London, this prawn version is our favourite recipe for *ceviche*. I make it quite often because my children love it so much. We eat it over corn *tostadas*, which are corn tortillas that have been fried or baked in the oven, topped with avocado and spicy salsa.

MAKES 8 TOSTADAS

360G PRAWNS, PEELED, CLEANED AND CUT INTO SMALL PIECES

150ML LIME JUICE

3 PLUM TOMATOES, FINELY DICED

½ ONION, FINELY DICED

20G FRESH CORIANDER, FINELY CHOPPED

1 TSP SEA SALT

FOR THE TOSTADAS

8 CORN TORTILLAS (SHOP-BOUGHT OR SEE PAGE 18 FOR HOMEMADE)

COOKING OIL SPRAY (OPTIONAL)

TO SERVE

MAYONNAISE

2 PERFECTLY RIPE HASS AVOCADOS, PEELED AND THINLY SLICED

SALSA MACHA (PAGE 140)

Put the prawns in a large bowl and pour the lime juice all over them, mixing well. Cover and place in the fridge to 'cook' in the lime juice for 40 minutes, taking them out a few times to mix well, so the prawns cook evenly.

Meanwhile, preheat the oven to 220°C (200°C fan/425°F/Gas 7) to make the tostadas.

Place the corn tortillas on a baking tray and spray with oil, if you like. Bake in the oven for about 20 minutes, flipping them halfway through, so they are hard and golden brown on both sides. Remove from the oven and place on a plate to cool.

When the prawns have turned pink, add the tomatoes, onion and coriander and season with salt. Combine well and put back in the fridge for 5 minutes.

To serve, spread some mayonnaise over a *tostada*, top it with prawn *ceviche* and then add some avocado slices and *salsa macha*.

LANGOSTA PUERTO NUEVO

PUERTO NUEVO-STYLE LOBSTER

Puerto Nuevo is a coastal town in Baja California – between Rosarito and Ensenada – that is famous for the amazing, locally caught lobsters. The popularity of this dish began in the 1950s, when the fishermen started cooking the lobsters for tourists visiting the town. Their way of cooking the lobster, by deep-frying them in pork lard, make the lobsters particularly tasty. Nowadays this way of cooking lobster is famous internationally.

It is an incredible experience to go and eat lobster in this part of the Baja Peninsula, as Puerto Nuevo is full of restaurants that specialize in this dish. If you go on a weekend, you'll need good luck to find a table, as it gets really busy, especially during the summer.

SERVES 4

4 SMALL LOBSTERS
1.5 LITRES SUNFLOWER OIL
1 TBSP SEA SALT
GROUND BLACK PEPPER

TO SERVE

1 LEMON, CUT INTO WEDGES
MELTED BUTTER
JUST-FRIED PINTO BEANS
  (PAGE 45)
RED RICE (PAGE 56)
10 FLOUR TORTILLAS (SHOP-
  BOUGHT OR SEE PAGE 16
  FOR HOMEMADE)
SPICY SALSA OF YOUR CHOICE
  (PAGES 136–145)

Ask your fishmonger to prepare the lobsters for you. Otherwise, to kill them humanely, place the lobsters in the freezer for 20 minutes then, using a very sharp knife, quickly plunge the knife down through the head. Remove the dark green parts of the flesh, cut in half lengthways and keep in the fridge, ready to fry.

Heat the sunflower oil in a large cast-iron pot or a deep-fat fryer big enough to fit a whole lobster. The oil needs to be between 180–190°C (356–374°F), so that the lobster fries quickly, but it does not burn.

Fry the lobster, meat-side down, for around 4 minutes. Remove it from the oil and drain any excess on kitchen paper. Season with a pinch of salt and pepper. Repeat with the remaining lobsters.

Serve with lemon wedges, melted butter, refried beans, tomato rice, flour tortillas and spicy salsa.

You can use lobster tails instead of a whole lobster. The amount of oil for this recipe refers to cooking small lobsters. If you are using bigger-sized lobsters, then use as much oil as you need for the lobster to be completely submerged.

TOSTADITAS DE CANGREJO

CRAB TOSTADITAS

This is a delicious and versatile recipe that can be served as a starter, over corn *tostaditas* or in a bowl with tortilla chips. Buying crab meat can be expensive, but it makes a great ingredient for special occasions.

MAKES 10 SMALL *TOSTADITAS*

200G WHITE CRAB MEAT

2 PLUM TOMATOES, DESEEDED AND FINELY DICED

2 SPRING ONIONS, FINELY CHOPPED

10G FRESH CORIANDER, FINELY CHOPPED

2 TBSP MAYONNAISE

1 TBSP MAGGI SAUCE

JUICE OF ½ LIME

½ TSP SEA SALT

TO SERVE

10 SMALL *TOSTADITAS*

SALSA MACHA (PAGE 140) (OPTIONAL)

Start by making the crab salad. In a large bowl, crumble up the crab meat. Then add the tomatoes, spring onions, coriander, mayonnaise, Maggi sauce, lime juice and salt. Mix well.

Cover the salad and let it rest in the fridge for at least 30 minutes before serving, so all the flavours have time to develop.

Preheat the oven to 220°C (200°C fan/425°F/Gas 7).

To make the *tostaditas*, use a round cookie cutter to cut out 10 small corn tortilla circles, approximately 6cm in diameter. Bake for around 15 minutes. Once golden brown, remove from the oven and set aside to cool.

When your *tostaditas* are ready, top with the crab mixture and add a few drops of *salsa macha* to each one – a bit of heat finishes them off nicely.

PULPO A LAS BRASAS

GRILLED OCTOPUS

My dad, who was a *costeñito* (a person from a coast town), would always bring a different type of seafood home. He was a very creative cook and octopus was something that he would make on special occasions. My mum, who is not very keen on fish or seafood, would complain but he'd always try to convince her to eat it. He'd say: 'Ay, Nery, *no sabes lo que es bueno!*', which means, 'No, Nery, you don't know what is good!'.

I know cooking octopus from scratch can be a bit scary, but don't be intimidated by the number of legs – it's very easy to cook.

SERVES 4

1.2KG OCTOPUS
3 BAY LEAVES
½ ONION
4 GARLIC CLOVES, PEELED
2 TBSP SEA SALT
OIL, FOR THE GRILL

FOR THE ADOBO SAUCE
2 GUAJILLO CHILLIES, STEMS
   REMOVED AND DESEEDED
1 ANCHO CHILLI, STEM REMOVED
   AND DESEEDED
240ML BOILING WATER
2 TBSP MAYONNAISE
1 TSP AMERICAN MUSTARD
1 TSP MAGGI SAUCE
1 TBSP WORCESTERSHIRE SAUCE
½ TSP SEA SALT
¼ TSP GROUND BLACK PEPPER
JUICE OF ½ LIME

TO SERVE
10 CORN TORTILLAS (SHOP-
   BOUGHT OR SEE PAGE 18 FOR
   HOMEMADE)
2 PERFECTLY RIPE HASS
   AVOCADOS, PEELED AND
   THINLY SLICED
2 LIMES, CUT INTO WEDGES
SALSA BANDERA (PAGE 28)
SPICY SALSA OF YOUR CHOICE
   (PAGES 136–145)
RED RICE (PAGE 56) (OPTIONAL)

Start by cooking the octopus. In a large saucepan, pour in enough water to cover the octopus. Add the bay leaves, onion, garlic and salt and bring to a steady simmer.

With a sharp knife, remove the eyes, the beak and the ink sac (if it has one). You can ask your fishmonger to do this for you, but you'll still need to wash the octopus in the sink when you take it home.

Hold the head and submerge it in the simmering pan of water for a few seconds, before removing. Repeat this three times. This process will make the tentacles curl, giving the octopus a nice shape. After shocking the octopus three times, leave it to cook in the water for 45 minutes, with the lid on.

While the octopus is cooking, make the *adobo* sauce. Rehydrate the guajillo and ancho chillies in hot water for 10 minutes. Remove them from the water and place in a blender, together with the mayonnaise, mustard, Maggi sauce, Worcestershire sauce, salt, pepper and lime juice. Blend until smooth and pass the *adobo* through a sieve to remove any bits. Pour the *adobo* into a bowl and set aside.

Once the octopus is cooked, remove from the hot water and leave to rest for 5 minutes until it's cool enough to handle. Separate the head with a sharp knife then, along with the tentacles, place in the bowl of *adobo*. Coat well with the sauce.

It's time to grill the octopus. Light up the grill and oil it lightly to prevent the octopus from sticking. Once the charcoal is ready, place the octopus on the grill and cook for about 3 minutes on each side. Use a cooking brush to coat with more *adobo*, if the octopus looks dry.
Take the octopus off the grill and separate the tentacles. These can be cut into small pieces, but they look more impressive when plated whole.

Serve with corn tortillas, avocado slices, lime wedges, red rice and *salsa bandera*, if you like.

Alternatively, the octopus can be cooked under the grill of an oven.

CAMARONES A LA DIABLA
DEVIL PRAWNS

We call this recipe *a la diabla* (devil) because the sauce is like fire; super spicy! If you are the type of person that can handle heat and likes spicy food, then this is the recipe for you, although you can adjust the heat level by adding more or fewer chillies. These prawns are usually served with rice and a simple green salad on the side.

Another popular way of cooking prawns is *camarones al ajillo*, where they are fried in garlic butter.

SERVES 4

2 PLUM TOMATOES
½ ONION
3 GARLIC CLOVES, PEELED
2 GUAJILLO CHILLIES, STEMS REMOVED AND DESEEDED
4 ARBOL CHILLIES, STEMS REMOVED AND DESEEDED
4 CHIPOTLES IN ADOBO
30G BUTTER
500G KING PRAWNS, PEELED, DEVEINED, HEADS REMOVED
½ TSP SEA SALT

TO SERVE
1 LEMON, CUT INTO WEDGES
GREEN SALAD
SPRING RICE (PAGE 55)
WARM CORN TORTILLAS (SHOP-BOUGHT OR SEE PAGE 18 FOR HOMEMADE)

In a saucepan, add the tomatoes, onion, garlic, guajillo and arbol chillies. Cover with 450ml water and bring to the boil. Reduce the heat and simmer for 10 minutes. Turn off the heat and set aside to cool.

Place the tomato and chillies mix in a blender with the chipotles in adobo. Blend until smooth before passing the sauce through a sieve, to remove any unwanted seeds or chilli peel.

Melt the butter in a frying pan over a medium heat. Add the prawns, season with salt and cook for 1 minute on each side. Add the *adobo* sauce and cook until hot.

Serve a portion of prawns with a lemon wedge, a green salad, spring rice and warm corn tortillas.

CHARALES FRITOS

FRIED LITTLE FISH

This is a dish I love to make on a summer's day as a snack or starter. My dad used to make it all the time at home. We would snack on little fried fish while he was prepping the bigger main meal, usually a red snapper which he would shallow-fry and we would eat with a fresh green salad and spring rice (page 55). If you can't find whitebait, you can use anchovies instead.

SERVES 4

1 LITRE SUNFLOWER OIL
180G PLAIN FLOUR
1 TSP SEA SALT
½ TSP GROUND BLACK PEPPER
⅛ TSP DRIED OREGANO
500G WHITEBAIT

TO SERVE
2 TBSP CHIPOTLE IN ADOBO PASTE
4 TBSP MAYONNAISE
1 LEMON, CUT INTO WEDGES

In a deep cast-iron pot, frying pan or deep-fat fryer, heat the oil to 190°C (374°F).

While the oil is getting hot, combine the flour, salt, black pepper and oregano in a bowl.

Put the whitebait on a plate and pat dry with kitchen paper to remove some of the moisture, then toss them in the flour. Shake well to remove any excess flour. Set aside and discard the used flour.

Once the oil has reached the right temperature, carefully drop in the whitebait and fry in batches for around 4 minutes until golden brown and crispy. Remove them from the oil and place on kitchen paper to drain.

Mix the chipotle in adobo paste with the mayonnaise and serve in a small bowl alongside the fish, together with the lemon wedges.

FILETE DE BACALAO CON HIERBAS FINAS

FRIED COD FILLETS IN HERB SAUCE

Here in London, I cook this for my family when I am in a hurry but not in the mood for pasta. All the ingredients can be easily found in the supermarket. Served *with arroz primavera* (spring rice, page 55), this has become my children's favourite fish dish.

SERVES 4

4 COD FILLETS, SKIN ON

60G PLAIN FLOUR

1 TSP SEA SALT

PINCH OF GROUND BLACK PEPPER

3 TBSP SUNFLOWER OIL

SPRING RICE (PAGE 55), TO SERVE

FOR THE HERB SAUCE

10G BUTTER

2 TBSP SUNFLOWER OIL

1 SHALLOT, FINELY CHOPPED

10 CHERRY TOMATOES, FINELY DICED

200ML WHITE WINE

10G FRESH CORIANDER, FINELY CHOPPED

20G FRESH FLAT-LEAF PARSLEY, FINELY CHOPPED

¼ TSP SEA SALT

To make the herb sauce, melt the butter and oil in a large frying pan over a medium–low heat and add the shallot. Fry for 2 minutes, making sure it doesn't burn. Then add the cherry tomatoes and fry for 3 minutes, stirring continuously. Pour in the white wine and increase the heat to high for one minute, to burn off the alcohol in the wine. Reduce the heat to low and add 50ml water, the coriander, parsley and salt. Cook for 2 minutes. Turn off the heat and set aside.

Before frying the fish, pat the cod fillets dry with kitchen paper. Set aside.

Mix the flour with the salt and ground black pepper and place on a plate. Dust the fillets with the flour and remove any excess.

Heat the oil in a non-stick frying pan over a medium–high heat. When the oil is hot, place the fillets skin-side down and fry for 2–3 minutes until the skin is golden. Then, using a spatula, turn the fillets to the other side and fry for a further 3 minutes.

Once the fish is cooked, reheat the herb sauce. Place the cooked fish in the sauce and transfer to a serving plate, pouring some more sauce on top. Accompany with spring rice.

PESCADO EMPAPELADO

SEA BASS IN PAPER

Perfect for a quick healthy dinner, any time of the year. Serve with white rice with sweetcorn (page 57) and *salsa bandera* (page 28) to make this recipe into a more substantial meal.

SERVES 4

2 TBSP AMERICAN OR DIJON MUSTARD

3 TBSP MAYONNAISE

PINCH OF GROUND BLACK PEPPER

½ TSP SEA SALT

2 WHOLE SEA BASS, DESCALED AND GUTTED

½ ONION, THINLY SLICED

½ GREEN BELL PEPPER, THINLY SLICED

2 PLUM TOMATOES, HALVED AND THINLY SLICED

TO SERVE

1 LEMON, CUT INTO WEDGES

WHITE RICE WITH SWEETCORN (PAGE 57)

SALSA BANDERA (SEE PAGE 28)

Preheat the oven to 220°C (200°C fan/425°F/Gas 7). Cut two pieces of baking parchment approximately 40cm long; large enough to wrap each individual fish.

Combine the mustard, mayonnaise, black pepper and salt and set aside in a bowl.

Open the fish and, with the help of a spoon, spread half of the mustard and mayonnaise mixture inside.

Divide the onion, pepper and tomatoes equally between the fish and place inside before closing the fish. Carefully place each fish in the centre of each piece of baking parchment and bring the edges together, scrunching to seal the parcel. Place on a baking tray and bake for 25 minutes.

Remove from the oven and open the parcels. The fish should still feel slightly firm.

Serve immediately. Garnish with lemon wedges and accompany the dish with sweetcorn rice and *salsa bandera*.

PESCADO ZARANDEADO

GRILLED BUTTERFLIED SEA BREAM

This technique for cooking fish was born in Nayarit, but it has become so popular that now every state has its own way to cook fish *zarandeado* style. This is an old method for grilling where the fish is butterflied, with the head on, before being cooked over charcoal.

Some recipes call for adding *achiote* (a red condiment from the Yucatán peninsula), others to add a mix of *chilli adobo*. I like this one, because it's made in the same way my dad used to make it when we hosted a *mariscada* (seafood party) at home. These types of parties are like a *carne asada* (page 132), but are usually held in places along the coast, where the seafood and fish is abundant and not too expensive. Once the fish is grilled, it is served on a platter and everyone helps themselves to tacos.

SERVES 4

2 WHOLE SEA BREAM, BUTTERFLIED WITH HEADS ON

3 TSP AMERICAN OR DIJON MUSTARD

110ML MAYONNAISE

½ TSP SEA SALT

PINCH OF GROUND BLACK PEPPER

1 TBSP MAGGI SAUCE

Ask your fishmonger to scale, gut and butterfly the fish, leaving the heads on.

Light up the barbecue and pile the coals onto one side until they are glowing red hot. At this stage, spread them around to create an even base, ready to grill the fish.

In a bowl, mix the mustard, mayonnaise, salt, black pepper and Maggi sauce. Spread this mixture over the fish before placing them onto a barbecue fish rack.

Grill the fish over the barbecue for about 8 minutes on each side. Alternatively, cook them in the oven at 220°C (200°C fan/425°F/Gas 7) for 15–20 minutes until the fish is cooked and the meat flakes easily from the bone.

Serve with lemon wedges, corn tortillas (page 18), just-fried pinto beans (page 45), *salsa bandera* (page 28) and a spicy salsa (pages 136–145).

CEVICHE DE ATÚN Y MANGO

TUNA & MANGO CEVICHE

In Mexico, there are many *ceviche* recipes and it seems as if every coastal state has its own way to prepare this delicious and popular dish. *Ceviche* is a fresh dish, perfect for a summer's day. The fish or seafood isn't cooked by heat, but instead is cooked in the acidity of the lime juice. I find this recipe is light and balanced; perfect as a starter or, if you make a big batch like we do at home, a healthy main course.

It is important to buy good-quality tuna or seafood to avoid food poisoning. Alphonso mangoes are perfect for this recipe, especially when they are in season. We always eat the *ceviche* with corn *tostadas* and a spicy shop-bought Mexican salsa, which pairs so well with the saltiness of seafood.

SERVES 4

250G SASHIMI-GRADE TUNA, FINELY DICED

¼ RED ONION, FINELY CHOPPED

150G PERFECTLY RIPE ALPHONSO MANGO, PEELED AND FINELY DICED

1 PERFECTLY RIPE HASS AVOCADO, PEELED AND FINELY DICED

5 SPRIGS OF FRESH CORIANDER, FINELY CHOPPED

1 FRESH JALAPEÑO OR SERRANO CHILLI, FINELY CHOPPED

1 TBSP MAGGI SAUCE

75ML LIME JUICE

½ TSP SEA SALT

TORTILLA CHIPS, TO SERVE

Finely dice the tuna and place in a large bowl. Add the red onion, mango, avocado, coriander and chilli. Mix well. Mix together the Maggi sauce with lime juice and pour this over the tuna. Season with salt and mix well.

Serve immediately with tortilla chips and some drops of shop-bought Mexican salsa.

TRIO DE CALDOS
THREE SPICED BROTHS Ⓥⓞ

Aguachile literally translates as 'chilli water'. This delicious way to eat seafood was born in Mazatlán, Sinaloa. Someone once told me that the original dish was made with beef and seasoned with *chiltepin*, a very spicy tiny chilli endemic from that region. Over the years, the recipe changed and people started to adapt the method for seafood. I am not sure if this story is true, but what I do know is that this way of eating seafood is my favourite and I highly recommend trying this recipe at home.

There are three main types of *aguachile*: green, red and black. The most popular recipe is made using prawns, but fresh fish or scallops can also be used, or even mushrooms for a vegan option.

The prawns are cooked in the chilli-lime juice and then garnished with red onion, cucumber, avocado and *chiltepin* chillies. They are usually eaten with corn *tostadas*. It's a perfect starter for a hot day.

AGUACHILE NEGRO

BLACK AGUACHILE

SERVES 2

120G PEELED PRAWNS, CLEANED, DEVEINED AND BUTTERFLIED

50ML WORCESTERSHIRE SAUCE

15ML MAGGI SAUCE

75ML LIME JUICE

30ML CLAMATO OR SPICED TOMATO JUICE

4 *CHILTEPINES* OR 6 BIRD'S EYE CHILLIES

GROUND BLACK PEPPER

35G CUCUMBER, PEELED AND THINLY SLICED

20G RED ONION, THINLY SLICED

2 DRIED *CHILTEPINES*, CRUSHED, OR ½ TSP DRIED CHILLI FLAKES

1 PERFECTLY RIPE HASS AVOCADO, PEELED AND THINLY SLICED

CORN *TOSTADAS* (PAGE 66) OR TORTILLA CHIPS

Put the prepared prawns in a bowl and store in the fridge while you make the *aguachile* (chilli-lime juice).

Using a blender, blend the Worcestershire sauce, Maggi sauce, lime juice, Clamato, chillies and a pinch of black pepper until smooth. Pass the sauce through a sieve, to remove any unwanted seeds or chilli peel.

Pour the *aguachile* over the prawns and return to the fridge for 30 minutes.

Once the prawns are pink, garnish with thin slices of cucumber, red onion and chiltepin or chilli flakes. Enjoy eating with thin slices of avocado and corn *tostadas* or tortilla chips.

Using oyster mushrooms makes a great vegan option.

AGUACHILE VERDE DE CAMARÓN

GREEN AGUACHILE

SERVES 2

120G PEELED PRAWNS, CLEANED, DEVEINED AND BUTTERFLIED

20G FRESH CORIANDER

2 SERRANO OR JALAPEÑO CHILLIES

150ML LIME JUICE

½ TSP SEA SALT

35G CUCUMBER, THINLY SLICED

20G RED ONION, THINLY SLICED

2 DRIED *CHILTEPINES*, CRUSHED, OR ½ TSP CHILLI FLAKES

1 PERFECTLY RIPE HASS AVOCADO AND PEELED, THINLY SLICED

TORTILLA CHIPS OR CORN *TOSTADAS* (PAGE 66)

Place the prepared prawns in a bowl and store in the fridge while you make the *aguachile* (chilli-lime juice).

Using a blender, blend the coriander, chillies, lime juice, salt and 50ml water until smooth. Pass the sauce through a sieve, to remove any unwanted seeds or chilli peel.

Pour the *aguachile* over the prawns and return to the fridge for 30 minutes.

Once the prawns are pink, garnish with thin slices of cucumber, red onion and *chiltepin* or chilli flakes. Enjoy eating with thin slices of avocado and corn *tostadas* or tortilla chips.

AGUACHILE ROJO

RED AGUACHILE

SERVES 2

120G PEELED PRAWNS, CLEANED, DEVEINED AND BUTTERFLIED

6 ARBOL CHILLIES

100ML LIME JUICE

100ML CLAMATO OR SPICED TOMATO JUICE

PINCH OF BLACK PEPPER

½ TSP SEA SALT

35G CUCUMBER, THINLY SLICED

20G RED ONION, THINLY SLICED

2 DRIED *CHILTEPINES*, CRUSHED, OR ½ TSP CHILLI FLAKES

1 PERFECTLY RIPE HASS AVOCADO, PEELED AND THINLY SLICED

CORN *TOSTADAS* (PAGE 66) OR TORTILLA CHIPS

Place the prepared prawns in a bowl and store in the fridge while you make the *aguachile* (chilli-lime juice).

Using a blender, blend the arbol chillies, lime juice, Clamato, black pepper and salt until smooth. Pass the sauce through a sieve, to remove any unwanted seeds or chilli peel.

Pour the *aguachile* over the prawns and return to the fridge for 30 minutes.

Once the prawns are pink, garnish with thin slices of cucumber, red onion and chiltepin or chilli flakes. Enjoy eating with thin slices of avocado and corn *tostadas* or tortilla chips.

ALBÓNDIGAS DE CAMARÓN

PRAWN BALLS SOUP

Originally, this dish is made with minced white fish. It is popular in the states of Baja California Sur and Sinaloa. At home, I like to make it using minced prawns combined with spices, sometimes with the addition of raw rice. The balls are cooked in a chilli-infused broth with vegetables, making it a delicious soup – perfect for a rainy day.

SERVES 4

FOR THE PRAWN BALLS
360G PRAWNS, PEELED, DEVEINED, HEADS REMOVED
10G FRESH CORIANDER
½ TSP SEA SALT
2 TBSP PANKO BREADCRUMBS

FOR THE BROTH
2 TBSP SUNFLOWER OIL
½ ONION, FINELY CHOPPED
2 GARLIC CLOVES, CRUSHED
3 PLUM TOMATOES, FINELY CHOPPED
1 TSP SEA SALT
1 TBSP CHIPOTLE IN ADOBO PASTE
2 CARROTS, PEELED AND CUT INTO 5MM ROUNDS
1 LARGE RED POTATO, PEELED AND CUT INTO 2CM DICE
12 GREEN BEANS, TRIMMED AND CUT INTO 2CM PIECES

TO SERVE
25G FRESH CORIANDER, CHOPPED
1 LIME, CUT INTO WEDGES

Start by making the prawn balls. Using a food processor, mince the peeled prawns, coriander, salt and breadcrumbs. Once done, place in a bowl.

Wet your hands slightly, so the prawn meat doesn't stick. Roll to make 30g balls; the mixture makes around 14 prawn balls in total. Rest in the fridge while making the broth.

To make the broth, heat the oil over a medium heat in a medium saucepan. Add the onion and fry for around 2 minutes until sweet and translucent. Add the garlic, followed by the tomatoes. Fry for 5–7 minutes until the tomatoes are soft.

Pour in 1 litre of water and add the salt and chipotle paste. Add more chipotle paste if you prefer it spicier. Bring to the boil and add the carrots and potato before reducing the heat, putting the lid on and simmering for 10 minutes.

Once the broth is cooked and ready, add the green beans and the prawn balls and simmer for 10 minutes.

Serve, garnished with coriander and a squeeze of lime juice.

This recipe can be made with another type of minced fish instead of the prawns, like cod, halibut, haddock or pollock.

CALDO DE SIETE MARES

FISH & SEAFOOD SOUP

This delicious soup is packed with amazing flavours; a wonderful choice for those cold nights when you fancy something comforting and cosy. The name *Siete Mares* (seven seas) is quite self-explanatory, as this soup contains many different types of fish and seafood. My dad used to make this soup during winter, as it was a great way to eat something fresh when we couldn't get outdoors. I make this with any type of seafood that I can find easily in the supermarket.

SERVES 4

12 RAW SHELL-ON PRAWNS

2 TBSP RAPESEED OIL

1 TBSP SEA SALT

½ TSP DRIED OREGANO

1 RED POTATO, PEELED AND CUT INTO 2CM DICE

3 CARROTS, PEELED AND CUT INTO 2CM DICE

1 GREEN BELL PEPPER, CUT INTO 2CM DICE

4 HADDOCK OR COD FILLETS, SKIN ON

250G MUSSELS, CLEANED AND DEBEARDED (PAGE 88)

250G CLAMS, CLEANED

1 COOKED OCTOPUS TENTACLE, CUT INTO CHUNKS

FOR THE GUAJILLO SAUCE

3 GUAJILLO CHILLIES, STEMS AND SEEDS REMOVED

240ML BOILING WATER

½ SMALL ONION, ROUGHLY CHOPPED

1 GARLIC CLOVE, PEELED

2 PLUM TOMATOES, ROUGHLY CHOPPED

2 TBSP TOMATO PURÉE

TO SERVE

CHOPPED FRESH CORIANDER

1 LIME, CUT INTO WEDGES

First make the guajillo sauce. Rehydrate the guajillos by placing them in the hot water for 10 minutes.

Once rehydrated, remove them from the water and place in a blender with the onion, garlic, tomatoes, tomato purée and 120ml of the guajillo soaking water. Blend until the mixture has a smooth consistency. Pass the sauce through a sieve, to remove any unwanted seeds or chilli peel. Set aside.

Move on to make the soup. Remove the prawn heads and peel the shell, tail and legs. Don't discard the heads and shells. Using a sharp knife, devein the prawns. Keep them in the fridge until you're ready to use later.

In a large saucepan, heat the oil over a medium heat and add the prawn heads and shells. Fry for 4 minutes, stirring constantly. Pour in the guajillo sauce and fry for 3 minutes.

Add 1 litre of water and the salt. Bring to the boil over a high heat, then reduce the heat and simmer for 10 minutes.

Strain the stock into a large bowl to remove the prawn heads and shells and discard.

Return the stock to the pan and add the oregano, potato, carrots and green pepper. Cook over a low heat for 10 minutes.

Put the fish chunks into the soup and cook for 5 minutes. Add the prawns, mussels, clams and octopus and cook for another 3 minutes. Turn off the heat and leave to rest for around 3 minutes before serving.

Serve in bowls, making sure to add a bit of everything to each one. Garnish with chopped coriander and finish with a squeeze of lime juice.

CAGUAMANTA

SKATE WING SOUP

SERVES 4

2 TBSP VEGETABLE OIL

½ SMALL WHITE ONION, FINELY CHOPPED

2 SMALL GARLIC CLOVES, CRUSHED

3 PLUM TOMATOES, FINELY CHOPPED

2 CARROTS, PEELED AND FINELY DICED

2 CELERY STICKS, FINELY DICED

1 GREEN BELL PEPPER, FINELY DICED

1½ TBSP SEA SALT

2 TBSP TOMATO PURÉE

50G PICKLED JALAPEÑOS, CHOPPED

1 TBSP PICKLED JALAPEÑO VINEGAR

1 BAY LEAF

PINCH OF GROUND BLACK PEPPER

½ TSP DRIED OREGANO

10 PITTED GREEN OLIVES, SLICED

2 SKATE WING FILLETS, CUT INTO 6 CHUNKS

TO SERVE

2 LIMES, CUT INTO WEDGES

CHOPPED FRESH CORIANDER

CHILTEPIN CHILLIES, CRUSHED (OPTIONAL)

A turtle species called *caguama* (loggerhead sea turtle) used to exist in abundance in the Baja Californian waters and were consumed by the natives of the region. Over time, this became a popular street food dish, and people used to cook *caguama* meat and make a soup with it. In time, sea turtles became endangered and since 1990 it is illegal to fish them. As an alternative, people have started to use skate wing.

The recipe varies from one state to another. In Sonora, they add prawns to the broth and in the Baja Peninsula, they only use skate wing. The meat can be served in a bowl as a soup, or served separately and eaten with corn tortillas. The combination of tomatoes, chillies and pickled jalapeños gives an almost sweet and sour flavour to the soup, which is perfect for the morning after a long night out.

At home in London, I like to cook this soup for my husband and use skate wings that are easily found in supermarkets or fishmongers. Ask your fishmonger to fillet them for you or – alternatively – cook in small pieces and remove the cartilage yourself, just before eating.

In a large saucepan, heat the vegetable oil over a medium heat, then add the onion and garlic. Fry for 2 minutes, making sure the garlic does not burn.

Add the chopped tomatoes and fry until they become soft. Reduce the heat and add the carrots, celery, green pepper and salt. Mix well, cover with a lid and simmer for 5 minutes.

Add the tomato purée, pickled jalapeños and their vinegar, a bay leaf, ground black pepper and oregano. Combine very well before pouring in 1 litre of water. Cover with a lid and bring to the boil over a high heat. Reduce the heat to low and simmer for 10 minutes.

Add the sliced olives and place in the pieces of skate wing. Cook for a further 10 minutes.

Serve in a bowl, making sure to get a piece of skate wing with some vegetables. Squeeze in some lime juice and add a handful of coriander, plus some *chiltepin* chillies if you like.

If you don't have a fishmonger to fillet the skate wings for you, you can cut them yourself into 3 pieces by following the line of the cartilage. Cook the pieces and then remove the meat in flakes with a spoon.

To make this recipe Sonoran style, add peeled prawns 3 minutes before turning the heat off and serve with shredded cabbage, chopped onion, lime juice and crushed *chiltepin* chilli.

CÓCTEL CAMPECHANO

SEAFOOD COCKTAIL

The term *campechano* is the name we give to a dish that has several ingredients belonging to one group. In this case, different types of seafood are used, but the term *campechano* can also apply to meat.

Some people know this recipe as a *vuelve a la vida* (come back to life) or *levanta muertos* (waking up the dead). This is because it is made using different types of seafood, making it quite substantial and reenergizing – perfect for curing a *cruda* (hangover). It is one of the most popular seafood cocktails in Mexico. I like to make it for a weekend lunch on a hot summer's day, together with some cold beers.

SERVES 4

12 RAW SHELL-ON PRAWNS

20 MUSSELS, CLEANED AND DEBEARDED (PAGE 88)

1 OCTOPUS TENTACLE, COOKED

8 OYSTERS

100G SASHIMI-GRADE TUNA

3 TBSP TOMATO KETCHUP

250ML CLAMATO OR SPICED TOMATO JUICE

150ML LIME JUICE

50ML WORCESTERSHIRE SAUCE

25ML MAGGI SAUCE

½ TSP SEA SALT

¼ TSP GROUND BLACK PEPPER

3 PLUM TOMATOES, FINELY DICED

1 ONION, FINELY CHOPPED

½ CUCUMBER, PEELED AND DESEEDED, FINELY DICED

SMALL BUNCH OF FRESH CORIANDER, FINELY CHOPPED

1 PERFECTLY RIPE HASS AVOCADO, FINELY DICED

Place the prawns, with their shell and heads on, in a saucepan and add 450ml water. Bring to the boil and cook for 6 minutes until pink.

Remove the prawns from the water to peel and remove their heads. Reserve the water, heads and shells for later. Set aside.

Return the prawn heads and shells to the water and continue cooking over a low heat for further 10 minutes. Turn off the heat and leave to cool.

To cook the mussels, place them in a saucepan and add a splash of water. Cover with a lid and let them cook over medium heat for around 5 minutes, until the mussel shells open. Remove the mussel meat from the shell and set aside. Discard any mussels that remain unopened.

Chop the octopus into small pieces, around 1cm in size. Carefully, open the oysters and remove them from their shells. Finely dice the tuna. Set aside.

In a bowl, mix the tomato ketchup, Clamato, lime juice, Worcestershire sauce, Maggi sauce, salt and black pepper.

In a large bowl, place all the seafood, the sauce and chopped vegetables. Add 120ml of the cold prawn cooking water and gently combine.

Serve in tall wide glasses, splash some *huichol* or *valentina salsa* (page 188) and enjoy with tortilla chips.

CÓCTEL DE MEJILLONES

MUSSELS COCKTAIL

When I was a child, Ensenada was a small coastal town with beautiful beaches. It still is, but it has grown a lot, over the years. I look back and remember driving in the car with my parents and siblings to find a nice rocky beach where we would spend the day. We'd play in the rock pools, jumping from one rock to another and picking sea anemones. My dad would venture into the rocks near the waves, to pick up mussels. He would collect as many as he could and we would come back home with a big bucket full of mussels, which we would eat for days, cooked in different ways. This is my favourite way to eat these delicious creatures of the sea.

SERVES 4

1KG MUSSELS

3 PLUM TOMATOES, FINELY DICED

½ SMALL ONION, FINELY CHOPPED

15G FRESH CORIANDER, CHOPPED

1 PERFECTLY RIPE HASS AVOCADO, PEELED AND FINELY DICED

1 TBSP WORCESTERSHIRE SAUCE

2 TBSP KETCHUP

200ML TOMATO JUICE OR CLAMATO

JUICE OF 3 LIMES

¼ TSP GROUND BLACK PEPPER

½ TSP SEA SALT

HUICHOL SALSA, TO SERVE (PAGE 188)

TOSTADAS, TO SERVE (PAGE 66) (OPTIONAL)

WATER BISCUITS, TO SERVE (OPTIONAL)

Clean the mussels under cold running water. Discard any that don't open or close when squeezed. Pull out the hairy 'beard' that sticks out from the shell, if it has one, then remove any barnacles with a knife and rinse again.

Place the mussels in a large pot and add 60ml water. With the lid on, cook them over a high heat for around 4 minutes until all the mussels have opened up. Turn the heat off and leave to cool.

Once cool, remove the mussel meat from the shells, discarding any that remain unopened.

Reserve the cooking juices from the pot and place the mussels in it so they stay hydrated.

In a large bowl, mix together the tomatoes, onion, coriander and avocado. Add the Worcestershire sauce, ketchup, tomato juice, lime juice, black pepper, salt and 200ml of the mussels' cooking juice.

Add the mussels and combine all the ingredients well. Cover and put in the fridge for 30 minutes.

Serve cold with some *huichol* salsa, *tostadas* or water biscuits in a tall glass or a bowl.

DIP DE ATÚN

TUNA & CHIPOTLE DIP

I have fond memories of my siblings and I sleeping under a table at a party, while my parents danced all night to the rhythm of Norteña or cumbia music. My parents used to bring blankets and we wouldn't leave the party until it was over, usually around 5 a.m.! Yes, parties in Mexico usually last all night long.

It was at one of those parties that I first tried this dip and I instantly loved it. It is a typical party canapé recipe that's remained popular. This creamy, delicious and nostalgic dip is very moreish. It is a simple recipe, but full of incredible flavours – believe me, when you learn how to make this, it will be a staple in your future party spreads.

SERVES 4

5 SHEETS OF GELATINE
145G CAN TUNA IN WATER
180G CREAM CHEESE
75ML DOUBLE CREAM
2 TBSP MAYONNAISE
35G WHITE ONION
2 CHIPOTLES IN ADOBO, WHOLE
PINCH OF GROUND BLACK PEPPER
1 TSP SEA SALT
RITZ CRACKERS, TO SERVE

Soak the gelatine sheets in 240ml cold water.

Put the tuna and it's juice from the can, in a blender. Add the cream cheese, double cream, mayonnaise, onion, chipotles, pepper and salt. Blend until smooth.

Once the gelatine is rehydrated, remove from the water and squeeze out any excess liquid.

Heat 100ml of water in a small saucepan over a low heat to dissolve the gelatine. Remove from the heat as soon as it has dissolved.

With the blender running, slowly pour in the liquid gelatine. When everything is properly combined, pour the tuna mixture into a mould and set in the fridge for at least 2 hours.

Unmould onto a serving plate and serve with Ritz crackers.

THE FLAVOURS FROM THE NORTH

The flavours of the north are unique; a mix of various cuisines, from the recipes of the indigenous groups who inhabit the region, to those that come from the various immigrants who have settled there, including Chinese, Jews and Mennonites. They have all shaped the way we eat.

BAJA CALIFORNIA

Baja California is located in the northwest of Mexico, bordering the American states of California and Arizona in the north, with Baja California Sur in the south. Its name and boundaries have been modified throughout its history. In 1824, Baja California was divided into *baja* (low) California and *alta* (high) California. The latter is now the state of California of the USA, lost in 1848 in the Guadalupe Hidalgo Treaty. In 1887, it was divided into two districts: Baja California Norte and Baja California Sur.

Because of its extensive coastline, with the Pacific Ocean on the west and the Sea of Cortez on the east, the gastronomy of this state revolves mostly around fish and seafood. It's very common among the locals to eat these for breakfast, like a *campechano* cocktail (seafood cocktail, page 86).

Baja California makes the most of its Mediterranean climate and amazing produce. So much so that a few years ago a new cuisine was born here. BajaMed is a concept that has influenced the cuisine of the region and become very popular. BajaMed is a fusion of three different cuisines: Mexican, Asian and Mediterranean. It combines traditional Mexican recipes with Chinese and Japanese ingredients and techniques, because of the large Chinese and Japanese community living in the area. Chefs and cooks of the region strongly believe in grow-it-yourself, responsibly foraging wild edible plants from the area, eating organic and local, and supporting small producers.

Tijuana is the city with the busiest border in the world, full of incredible places to eat and the birthplace of the Caesar Salad. If you want to eat the best Chinese food in Mexico, head to Mexicali, which has a large Chinese community; La Chinesca. This is Mexicali's Chinatown, famous for its incredible food. La Rumorosa, the motorway that leads to Mexicali, is well known for its altitude and amazing views.

BAJA CALIFORNIA SUR

At the south of the peninsula lies Baja California Sur. With its beautiful, clear, turquoise beaches and lovely weather, this region is a paradise for those who want to enjoy a nice time in the sun.

It is the leading salt producer in Mexico, and the biggest salt factory in the world is in Guerrero Negro, in Mulegé, producing around 7 million tons of salt per year. Also in this area is the town of Ojo de Liebre, where every year a big pod of grey whales migrates to the waters to give birth.

The state is full of little old towns, full of incredible history, like Loreto or San Ignacio. The Vizcaino desert is right in the centre of this region, where you can find the most stunning and interesting vegetation, including cacti as tall as buildings. Because of its location, people's diets are full of seafood and fish and one of the most popular dishes are fish balls.

CHIHUAHUA

The biggest place in Mexico is Chihuahua. Bigger than the UK, its name means 'lady of the desert'. Bordering Texas and New Mexico to the north, it contains the largest desert area in Mexico, with the Chihuahua desert covering most of the state and other neighbouring states, too. If you ever have the opportunity to visit this wonderful place, you need to visit *Las Barracas del Cobre* (Copper Canyon), which offers breathtaking views.

Because of the extreme weather in Chihuahua, a lot of the produce in the region is dehydrated to preserve it for longer, including fruits, vegetables and meat. A group who has contributed to the region's cuisine are the Mennonites, who settled in Chihuahua in 1922. Mainly from Holland and Germany, they came fleeing the pressure of the English Crown to provide military service. Most still live in the town of Cuauhtémoc, where they produce their own food. The cheeses that they make are a staple of the cuisine in Chihuahua.

COAHUILA

If you want to eat the best *asado de puerco*, a dish made with tender pieces of pork, cooked in a dark red sauce of dried chillies and spices, you have to go to Coahuila. It's a state in the central part of Northern Mexico, bordering Texas to the north.

Coahuila is famous for its desserts and sweets made with walnuts, like *empanadas* or *pastel de nuez* (walnut cake), because in Coahuila, like Chihuahua, is one of the main walnut producers in Mexico. In this region, they also make flour tortillas that can be savoury or sweet. And we can't talk about Coahuila without mentioning that this is where one of the most well-known Mexican dishes is from: *nachos* were created in the town of Piedras Negras!

Parras de la Fuente is well known because of its wineries; the Casa Madero is the first winery established in Latin America and they also hold a Wine Fair every year. Viesca, Candela and Guerrero are some of the picturesque cities that you can visit. Cuatro Ciénegas is a must while visiting Coahuila, especially if you are a nature lover.

NUEVO LEÓN

In the northeast, you'll find Nuevo León, the land of *cabrito* (kid goat), known as one of the richest states in the country due to its infrastructure for industry and commerce. Life in Nuevo León is fast, especially in the capital city Monterrey, the third most populated city in Mexico.

When it comes to food, people love to sit down and take their time. The most popular dish is *cabrito*, which can be cooked in different ways, but the most traditional is on a spit, the whole carcass is opened flat and speared on the spit, then placed next to a bed of glowing coals and roasted slowly and served with corn tortillas and spicy salsa. This dish has its roots in the cuisine of the Sephardic Jews who settled in Nuevo León around the 1500s.

SINALOA

The best seafood dishes in the north come from Sinaloa, due to its extensive coastline. The land of the *aguachile*, a dish made with fresh prawns cooked in a very spicy lime juice, is also known for its great meat dishes like *chilorio* (shredded pork in adobo) or *machaca* (dried meat). The region also has a wide variety of *tamales*, like the *tamales barbones*, a *tamal* with a whole prawn in it, *tamales de elote*, corn *tamales*, which are usually sweet or a combination of sweet and savoury.

This is one of my favourite places in the north of Mexico because my mum was born there and I've spent so much time exploring it, especially Culiacán, the capital. Mazatlán, a coastal city, is one of those places that cannot be missed. I love the *ceviche* from Sinaloa because the seafood is so fresh and the combinations are mind-blowing. During the summer, people drink barley water and *horchata*, as well as the local Pacifico beers. There are a lot of small, picturesque towns to visit, like Mocorito, El Fuerte and El Rosario.

SONORA

A state located in the northwest of Mexico, near to Arizona and New Mexico (USA), Hermosillo, the capital, is a beautiful city. The buildings' façades in the city centre are breathtaking and transport you back in time. Other towns worth a visit include San Carlos and Puerto Peñasco, both near the sea.

Sonora is the land of the *tortillas de harina* (flour tortillas), which you must try if visiting. This is the home of the red gold, the *chiltepin* chilli. It is common to find a lot of places that sell *burritos* or *tacos de carne asada* (steak tacos), which is the speciality of the state, as well as *machaca* (shredded dried meat).

DURANGO

Located in the northwest of Mexico, below Chihuahua, you can find Durango, a picturesque land of natural beauty and home to one of the most beautiful cathedrals in the north of Mexico.

Just like its neighbour state Chihuahua, Durango has extreme weather. In the summer it's very hot but the winters are really cold, so the first settlers used to dry or make preserves with fresh ingredients to be consumed throughout the year. Although nowadays circumstances are different, people are still very attached to these traditions and this shows in the way they cook and the ingredients they use. For example, *chile pasado*, a dried chilli made using a long green pepper, typical of the region, is dried using a special method and utilized in many traditional dishes.

TAMAULIPAS

Tamaulipas is located next to the Gulf of Mexico, at the far end of the northeast of the republic, with Ciudad Victoria as its capital. Tampico is one of the most important cities of the state with beautiful French and New Orleans-style buildings. Aldama, another city not far from Tampico, is perfect for those who love nature. There you can find the deepest *cenote*, a natural underground water reservoir, in the world. Jaumave, a city on the north of Tamaulipas, is a place with incredible crystal-clear rivers where you can spend the day with the family. Like these cities, there are many more places in the state with breathtaking scenery.

When I think of the food in Tamaulipas, I think about all the mouthwatering crab dishes, including *salpicón* (a cold dish salad made with shredded meat and mixed with vegetables), *quesadillas* and cocktails, or the super creamy oysters eaten just with some sort of spicy salsa.

DEL RANCHO

FROM THE RANCH

Meat plays a very important part in the life of any *Norteño* (northerner). With its dry terrain, the north is perfect for raising cattle. This is our most famous product. Every northern family loves throwing a good *carne asada* (barbecue), gathering people for a *cabrito* or organizing a proper *discada Norteña* (another type of northern barbecue). When our weather allows it, we don't need much of an excuse to light up the *asador* (barbecue), open some beers, play some music and start a party.

In the north of Mexico, the most popular way to celebrate something is always organizing a *carne asada* (page 132). Sometimes, when my dad was in the mood to *tirar la casa por la Ventana* (to spare no expense), he would make a proper lamb *barbacoa* (lamb in the oven) by digging a hole in our front garden, filling it with charcoal and burying a pot full of lamb pieces marinated in adobo until the next day.

I can clearly remember the commotion as the pot was lifted out – my God! The deep, spicy aromas coming out of that pot were heavenly, the meat was so tender that it would fall from the bone easily. My mum would have everything ready on the table: corn tortillas, pinto beans, salsas, garnishes. We would all gather and devour the *barbacoa* in no time at all, soon to fall into a food coma of pure happiness. I loved those simple moments with my family. We were all together – just talking about mundane things or listening to music. The adults would be drinking beers and the children usually running around, making a racket.

In this chapter, I've included all my favourite meat dishes – some have been in our family for a long time and they are all special recipes that I cook over and over again.

BIRRIA DE RES

BEEF BIRRIA

SERVES 4

2 TBSP SUNFLOWER OIL

1KG BRAISING STEAK OR BEEF SHIN, CUT INTO 5CM CUBES

3 BONE MARROW DISCS OR A LARGE BONE MARROW

2 BAY LEAVES

FOR THE ADOBO

5 GUAJILLO CHILLIES, CLEANED, STEMS REMOVED AND DESEEDED

3 ARBOL CHILLIES (OPTIONAL, FOR EXTRA HEAT)

2 PLUM TOMATOES, CUT INTO CHUNKS

1 ONION, CUT INTO CHUNKS

4 GARLIC CLOVES, PEELED

½ TSP DRIED OREGANO

½ TSP GROUND CUMIN

½ TSP GROUND CINNAMON

½ TSP GROUND GINGER

2 CLOVES

3 BLACK PEPPERCORNS

1 TBSP WHITE WINE VINEGAR

20G SEA SALT

TO SERVE

SMALL BUNCH OF FRESH CORIANDER, CHOPPED

½ ONION, FINELY CHOPPED

2 LIMES, CUT INTO SMALL WEDGES

RED SALSA (PAGE 145)

WARM CORN TORTILLAS (SHOP-BOUGHT OR SEE PAGE 18 FOR HOMEMADE)

The word *birria* in colloquial Spanish means 'bad/ugly' or 'something of little value'. This recipe was created for the poor, who cooked *birria* using the cuts that nobody wanted.

The original *birria* (goat broth) recipe is from the state of Jalisco, where it's cooked with a mixture of dried chillies, spices and vegetables. More recently, the *birria* cooked in Tijuana has become very well known among the Mexican foodies – some say that it has surpassed in flavour the *birria* from Jalisco. Although the original recipe for *birria* is made with goat meat, nowadays, beef is widely used as it is easier to source. A delicious broth, cooked for hours, it is just heavenly.

Depending on how much time I have; I make it either in the oven, which takes a bit longer, or over the hob, where I have a better control of the consistency. It's a perfect dish for a gathering with friends or for a Sunday brunch – or why not eat it like Mexicans do, for breakfast?

You can make the *adobo* a day in advance to save time. To do this, start by heating a frying pan over a medium heat and lightly toasting the chillies, making sure not to burn them.

Place the chillies in a saucepan, add the tomatoes, onion and garlic. Cover with water, bring to the boil, then reduce the heat and cook for 5 minutes. Set aside to cool.

Once cool, remove the vegetables and chillies from the saucepan, put them in a blender, adding 100ml of their cooking water, plus all the dried spices, the wine vinegar and salt. Blend until smooth. Sieve the adobo, to remove any large bits, and reserve the stock to make the *birria*.

Start making the *birria*. Heat the oil over medium heat in a large cast-iron pot and brown the meat in batches. Place the meat back into the pot and add the bone marrow discs and bay

leaves. Pour in the *adobo* and 1.5 litres of water. Bring to the boil over hight heat, then reduce to a simmer, covering with a lid. Cook for around 2 hours, or until the meat is tender enough to fall apart easily. Make sure to check from time to time, topping up with more water if necessary. Once the meat is cooked, remove it from the broth and shred. Discard the bone marrow discs and the bay leaves.

To serve, you can either place some shredded meat in a bowl, pour over some broth and garnish with chopped coriander, onion, a squeeze of lime juice and some spicy salsa or take some meat out, heat some corn tortillas and make *birria tacos*, serving the broth in a cup.

Alternatively, you can drench a corn tortilla in the broth, heat in a frying pan, fill with cheese and make *quesa birrias*.

To make the birria spicier, add some arbol chillies. Portobello mushrooms make a good vegan option, and take less time to cook.

BARBACOA SINALOENSE

SINALOA-STYLE LAMB BARBACOA

SERVES 6

1.2KG LAMB LEG ON THE BONE

2 FRESH BAY LEAVES

1 ONION, SLICED

1 ANAHEIM OR TURKISH 'YESIL TATLI BIBER' LONG GREEN PEPPER, DESEEDED AND THINLY SLICED

330ML LAGER

2 TBSP SEA SALT

25 BABY POTATOES

FOR THE ADOBO

3 GUAJILLO CHILLIES, CLEANED, SEEDS AND STEMS REMOVED

2 PASILLA CHILLIES, CLEANED, SEEDS AND STEMS REMOVED

2 PLUM TOMATOES, CUT INTO CHUNKS

½ ONION, CUT INTO CHUNKS

5 GARLIC CLOVES, PEELED

½ TBSP CUMIN SEEDS

1 CLOVE

4 BLACK PEPPERCORNS

2 TBSP WHITE WINE VINEGAR

TO SERVE

15 WARM CORN TORTILLAS (SHOP-BOUGHT OR SEE PAGE 18 FOR HOMEMADE)

PINTO BEANS FROM THE POT (PAGE 22) (OPTIONAL)

RED RICE (PAGE 56) (OPTIONAL)

SMALL BUNCH OF FRESH CORIANDER, FINELY CHOPPED

1 SMALL ONION, FINELY CHOPPED

2 LIMES, CUT INTO WEDGES

RED SALSA (PAGE 145)

Barbacoa is a technique used to cook meat underground. The word comes from the Mayan word *baalbak*, which means 'meat covered with earth'. It is one of the more challenging recipes from this book – not because it is complicated to cook – but because the meat needs a lot of time in the oven to be perfectly cooked.

In Mexico, the best *barbacoas* come from Hidalgo, a state in east central Mexico. Here, the pieces of meat are seasoned with salt, then placed in an underground hole, lit with wood and wrapped in maguey leaves. A pot is placed underneath the pieces of lamb, with water, rice, onion, chickpeas and other ingredients, so the fat from the meat drops into it, enhancing the flavour of the broth. The hole is sealed with clay and the whole thing is left to cook for 24 hours. The result is a very tender and juicy meat and a mouth-watering broth.

My recipe is not overly complicated, as it is done in the oven. Make sure when taking it out that the meat is properly tender. I would suggest cooking it for an alternative Sunday roast or for a party to celebrate a special occasion.

To make the adobo, first place the chillies in a saucepan, add the tomatoes, onion, garlic and 450ml water. Bring to the boil, then reduce the heat and simmer for 10 minutes. Turn off the heat and leave to cool.

Once cool, remove the chillies and vegetables from the water, reserving for later use, and place them into a blender. Add the cumin seeds, clove, peppercorns and vinegar. Blend until smooth. Sieve the sauce to remove any bits. Set aside.

Preheat the oven to oven to 220°C (200°C fan/425°F/Gas 7).

Move on to make the barbacoa. Cut the lamb into big chunks, approximately 7cm in size. Place the meat, bones and all, into a casserole dish or a Dutch oven. Add the adobo, half of the reserved chilli water, the bay leaves, onion, Anaheim green pepper, lager and salt. Mix well. Put on the lid on and cook for 20 minutes, then reduce the oven temperature to 180°C and cook for 2 hours.

Halfway through, remove the casserole from the oven to check if it needs water. If it does, top up with 250ml of hot water. Add the baby potatoes before covering again and returning to the oven for a further 40 minutes.

The *barbacoa* is ready when the meat is tender and falls from the bone easily.

Serve the baby potatoes on a platter. Take the pieces of lamb and shred the meat, so that people can serve themselves. Let everyone help themselves by preparing the *barbacoa* as a *tacos*: warm corn tortillas, a bit of beans, a bit of rice, a baby potato, shredded lamb, coriander, onion, squeeze of lime juice and some spicy salsa.

BISTEC RANCHERO

BAVETTE STEAK WITH VEGETABLES

This quick, easy and flavoursome dish is my mum's favourite recipe to make when short on time. It is a traditional recipe from the north of Mexico; some people add potatoes, others blend the tomatoes, but the one thing that all recipes have in common is that they all use good-quality steak. In this case I've used *arrachera,* bavette steak, which is an inexpensive cut that's juicy and flavoursome. It's always served with refried pinto beans and flour or corn tortillas.

In Guadalupe Valley, one of the wine regions of Baja California, there is a restaurant that serves *bistec ranchero* (ranch-style steak) for breakfast with fried eggs, refried beans and flour tortillas. At home, I sometimes make this for an easy midweek dinner.

SERVES 4

1 GREEN BELL PEPPER

3 TBSP RAPESEED OR SUNFLOWER OIL

1 ONION, SLICED

650G BAVETTE STEAK, CUT INTO SMALL THIN STRIPS

2 GARLIC CLOVES, FINELY CHOPPED

4 PLUM TOMATOES, ROUGHLY CHOPPED

1 JALAPEÑO, WHOLE

1 TSP SEA SALT

¼ TBSP GROUND BLACK PEPPER

TO SERVE

JUST-FRIED PINTO BEANS (PAGE 45)

FLOUR TORTILLAS (SHOP-BOUGHT OR SEE PAGE 16 FOR HOMEMADE)

Char the green pepper over a gas hob or under the grill. Once evenly charred, place the pepper in a zip-lock plastic bag for 10 minutes to sweat. Remove the burnt skin and seeds before cutting into 3cm-long strips. Set aside.

Heat the oil in a large frying pan over a medium heat and add the onion and garlic. Fry for 2 minutes, mixing continuously to avoid burning. Add the bavette strips and mix well. Fry for 5 minutes. Add the tomatoes, green pepper and the jalapeño. Season with the salt and black pepper.

Add 5 tablespoons of water. Mix very well, reduce the heat, cover with a lid and simmer for 10 minutes. Once the vegetables and the steak are cooked, serve with some fried beans and flour tortillas. The cooked jalapeño can be served to the one person in the family that loves an extra kick in their food – in our case, it was always my dad.

POZOLE ROJO DE POLLO

CHICKEN RED HOMINY SOUP

Pozole is made with a special type of corn grain that we call *cacahuazintle*, or *maiz pozolero*. The name of the dish derives from the Nahuatl word 'pozolli', which means 'sparkling'. Popular all around Mexico, it is believed that *pozole* was consumed way before the Spaniards arrived and was often made as an offering to Xochiquetzal, the god of fertility.

Nowadays, *pozole* is made for national celebrations, like Independence Day or Day of the Dead. However, its versatility means it's also great to make on a sick day to clear a cold. There are three types of *pozole* variations: white, green and red. The red version is very common in the north of Mexico as the guajillo chillies used in the broth make a distinctive bright red colour.

SERVES 4

3 PLUM TOMATOES, HALVED

1 SMALL ONION, PEELED AND HALVED

6 GARLIC CLOVES, PEELED

2 TBSP SEA SALT

1 TSP DRIED OREGANO

4 CHICKEN LEGS, SKIN ON

6 GUAJILLO CHILLIES, CLEANED, SEEDS AND STEMS REMOVED

830G CAN PRE-COOKED HOMINY, RINSED

TO SERVE

¼ ICEBERG LETTUCE, FINELY SHREDDED

1 SMALL ONION, FINELY CHOPPED

10 RADISHES, THINLY SLICED

DRIED OREGANO

CRUSHED *CHILTEPINES* OR BIRD'S EYE CHILLIES

2 LIMES, CUT INTO WEDGES

Put the tomatoes, onion, garlic, salt, oregano, chicken legs and 2 litres of water in a large cast-iron pot or saucepan. Bring to the boil over a high heat. Remove any scum that forms on top before reducing the heat, covering with a lid and cooking over a low heat for 30 minutes.

Remove the chicken from the broth to avoid over-cooking. Add the guajillo chillies to the broth for 10 minutes to rehydrate. Then remove them from the broth together with onion, garlic and tomatoes and put in a blender to blend until smooth. Sieve the sauce over the broth, this will get rid of anything that didn't blend properly and create a smoother sauce.

At this stage, add the hominy and cook for 30 minutes, or until the grains are soft. Shred the chicken and return to the broth for the last 10 minutes of cooking.

Serve with a little of each topping, finishing with a squeeze of lime.

My version uses pre-cooked *cacahuazintle*, which I buy from an online Mexican shop specialist.

TAMALES ESTILO SINALOA

SINALOA-STYLE TAMALES

In Mexico, we have made *tamales* for centuries. A *tamal* is a parcel made with nixtamalized corn dough. The dough is spread on a dried corn husk or banana leaf, then a filling is added — normlly a meat or vegetable stew — and it is wrapped and steamed until the dough is cooked. In my Great-grandma's recipe below, the dough is infused with a guajillo sauce, giving the dough a beautiful red colour.

Making *tamales* is quite labour intensive, which is the main reason Mexicans make plenty at one time. They are a celebration dish made on special occasions. I grew up making this recipe every single year to celebrate Christmas Eve. My whole family would participate: my mum made the dough, my dad would make the filling, one of my sisters would cut the vegetables. Then, when everything was ready, we would gather around the table and start a conveyor belt process: my mum would spread the dough onto the husk, my dad would add the filling, then my sister the vegetables, my other sister would close them and my brother and I would tie them. Making *tamales* together is an incredible family affair and is my dearest Mexican food memory of all — one that always brings tears to my eyes, every time I think of it.

MAKES 18

FOR COOKING THE MEATS
350G BEEF BRISKET, CUT INTO CHUNKS
400G PORK SHOULDER, CUT INTO 2 PIECES
2 PLUM TOMATOES, HALVED
½ ONION, PEELED
2 GARLIC CLOVES, PEELED
2 TBSP SEA SALT

FOR THE MEAT STEW
2 GUAJILLO CHILLIES, CLEANED, STEMS REMOVED AND DESEEDED
2 TBSP VEGETABLE OIL
½ ONION, THINLY SLICED
2 PLUM TOMATOES, FINELY DICED
½ GREEN PEPPER, THINLY SLICED

FOR THE EXTRA INGREDIENTS
18 LARGE, DRIED, CORN HUSK LEAVES FOR TAMALES, PLUS 36 CORN HUSK STRINGS
1 SMALL RED POTATO
1 CARROT
½ COURGETTE
18 PITTED GREEN OLIVES
10 PICKLED JALAPEÑOS (OPTIONAL)

FOR THE TAMAL DOUGH
400ML MEAT BROTH
3 GUAJILLO CHILLIES
500G TAMAL FLOUR OR MASA HARINA (GMO-FREE CORN FLOUR)
1 TSP BAKING POWDER
1½ TBSP FINE SALT
140G WARM MELTED PORK LARD OR SUNFLOWER OIL
300ML WARM WATER

Continues overleaf

First cook the meat by putting the beef and pork, tomatoes, onion, garlic and salt in a cast-iron pot, and covering with 2 litres of water. Bring to the boil over a high heat. Remove any scum that forms on the surface. Once it starts to boil, reduce the heat and cover with a lid before leaving to simmer for 2 hours.

When the meat is cooked and tender, remove (reserving the broth for later use) and leave to cool. Shred and cut into small pieces before setting aside.

Pass the broth through a sieve and reserve for use in the stew and the dough.

To make the stew, put 200ml of the hot meat broth into a jug and soak the guajillo chillies for 10 minutes. Once softened, put them in a blender with the broth and blend until smooth. Pass the sauce through a sieve to remove any unwanted seeds or chilli peel.

In a large frying pan, heat the vegetable oil over a medium heat, add the sliced onion, diced tomatoes and sliced green pepper. Fry for about 3 minutes, stirring from time to time. Once the vegetables are partly cooked, add the shredded meat, followed by the guajillo sauce. Reduce the heat and simmer for 5 minutes. Turn off the heat and set aside.

Meanwhile, soak the corn husk leaves in hot water for around 15 minutes. Separate the large leaves from the small ones. You will use the large leaves to wrap the tamales and the small ones to make strings.

Peel and cut the potato lengthways to make thin 4cm-long sticks, then place in a bowl and cover with water so they don't darken. Cut the carrot the same way, covering with water as well so it doesn't dry out. Cut the courgette into thin 4cm-long strips and place in a bowl. Slice the olives and jalapeños, if using.

To make the tamal dough, put 200ml meat broth in a jug and soak the guajillo chillies for 10 minutes to soften. Once softened, put them in a blender with the broth and blend until smooth. Pass the sauce through a sieve and set aside.

Place the tamal flour in a large bowl, add the baking powder and salt and mix well. Then add the melted lard or sunflower oil and combine well until the flour has absorbed all liquid.

Add the guajillo sauce and mix well, follow by the warm water and the remaining meat broth. Mix well until the dough comes together.

It's time to start making the tamales. Grab a soaked corn husk leaf, place it on the worktop with the smoother side facing upwards. The easiest way to spread the dough over the corn husk is by making a 70g dough ball and thinly spreading it over the centre of the leaf by hand.

Add around 1 tablespoon of meat stew (around 40g), a stick of each vegetable, one olive, plus a jalapeño slice if you want to add some heat. Wrap the dough with the corn husk leaf and tie a knot at each end, using the short corn husk leaves.

Repeat the process until all the dough has been used.

Once all the tamales are done, they need to be steamed to cook the dough. If you don't own a tamalera (special pot for tamales), a steamer can be used – or a metal steamer basket. Whichever you choose, make sure it's big enough to fit all the tamales.

Pour 1.5 litres of hot water in the tamalera or a large cast-iron pot, place in the metal steamer basket and arrange the tamales on top of each other. Put the lid on and seal with foil. Steam the tamales over a low heat for 1 hour. Turn the heat off and let the tamales set and cool for 20 minutes.

Remove the foil and take a tamal, discarding the corn husk leaf before eating. Serve together with Frijoles Puercos (page 23) and a green salad for a proper Sinaloa-style feast.

To save time, you can cook the meat and make the stew a day or two before constructing. You can even store these elements in the freezer, just as long as you remember to defrost properly before making the tamales. To make this recipe vegetarian, replace the meat with some shredded oyster mushrooms and the broth with vegetable stock.

EMPANADAS BAJA CALIFORNIANAS

SHREDDED BEEF EMPANADAS

The first time I tried these *empanadas*, I was a little girl – and the flavour stayed somewhere deep in my subconscious. A few years ago, my family and I took a road trip down south of the Baja Peninsula and stopped in La Paz, where my Auntie Toña lives. She took us to this incredible place for breakfast, in the middle of the desert. She ordered the house *empanadas* for us to eat. Believe me when I say that I jumped with happiness. I told her the story of eating them as a child and how I'd never found them again. That day, I ate quite a few!

When I came back to London, I was on a mission to find the recipe – and here it is. Instead of using puff or shortcrust pastry, I use a similar dough that is used for flour tortillas. When the *empanada* is fried, it results in this super thin, crunchy casing. For a vegetarian alternative, replace the beef with sweet refried beans.

MAKES 15

FOR THE BRISKET
750G BEEF BRISKET, CUT INTO 2 BIG PIECES
½ ONION, PEELED
2 GARLIC CLOVES, PEELED
1 TOMATO, HALVED
1 TBSP SEA SALT
3 DRIED GUAJILLO CHILLIES, CLEANED, SEEDS AND STEMS REMOVED

FOR THE BEEF FILLING
3 TBSP VEGETABLE OIL
1 SMALL ONION, THINLY SLICED
½ ANAHEIM OR TURKISH 'YESIL TATLI BIBER' GREEN PEPPER, OR GREEN BELL PEPPER, SLICED
1 LARGE RED POTATO, PEELED AND CUT INTO 1CM CUBES
GUAJILLO SAUCE (SEE ABOVE)
SHREDDED BEEF BRISKET (SEE ABOVE)
180G PITTED GREEN OLIVES, HALVED
1 TBSP SEA SALT

FOR THE DOUGH
500G PLAIN WHITE FLOUR, PLUS EXTRA FOR DUSTING
1 TSP TABLE SALT
1 TSP CASTER SUGAR
50G VEGETABLE SHORTENING OR GOOD-QUALITY PORK LARD, MELTED
1 SMALL EGG, WHISKED, AT ROOM TEMPERATURE
200ML WARM WATER

FOR THE EXTRA INGREDIENTS
400ML SUNFLOWER OIL
CHARRED SALSA, TO SERVE (PAGE 138)

Continues overleaf

First cook the brisket. Place the beef in a large saucepan. Add the onion, garlic, tomato and salt and cover with water. Bring to the boil, removing any scum that forms on top, then reduce the heat and cook for around 1 hour until the meat is tender.

Remove the meat (reserving 250ml of broth to use later), place on a plate and leave to cool. Once cool, shred the brisket into small pieces. Set aside. This step can be done in advance and kept in the fridge until ready to use.

To make the guajillo sauce, place the guajillos in a jar and cover with hot water. Leave them to soak for 10 minutes until soft. Blend the guajillos with the same tomato, onion and garlic that was used to cook the brisket. Add the reserved beef brisket stock. Set aside.

To make the beef filling, heat the oil over a medium heat in a cast-iron pot or medium saucepan. Add the onion and fry for 2 minutes, followed by the green pepper and diced potato. Continue frying for 5 minutes. Add the guajillo sauce, together with the shredded beef and green olives. Lower the heat, cover with a lid and cook the stew for 10 minutes until the potatoes are soft. Turn the heat off and set aside to cool.

To make the dough, place the flour, salt and sugar in a large bowl. Pour the melted shortening into the dry ingredients and mix well. Add the egg and water and combine. Once a dough has formed, knead it on the worktop until it is smooth and bounces back when pressed. Make 15 dough balls of equal size. Place them back in the bowl, cover with a tea towel and leave to rest for 10 minutes.

Once the beef filling is cold and the dough has rested, it is time to make the empanadas. Lightly dust a worktop with flour. Using a rolling pin, work each dough ball into a round tortilla about 18 to 20cm wide. Place 2 tablespoons of the beef filling in one half of the tortilla and fold in half.

To seal the empanada, starting crimping the edges from one end, making little folds all the way around. Have a baking tray ready with a clean tea towel on it. One by one, place each empanada on the tea towel as you contiue to make the rest. Repeat with the remaining dough and filling.

Heat the sunflower oil in a large frying pan over a medium–high heat. Once the oil has reached 180°C (356°F), start frying the empanadas, making sure not to overcrowd the frying pan. Fry on one side for 2 minutes, or until golden brown, then flip to cook the other side for 2 minutes.

Once all the empanadas are fried, pat with kitchen paper to remove any excess oil. Serve with charred salsa.

To save time, you can cook the brisket and make the filling a day or two before and keep in the fridge. A good vegetarian alternative for the beef is to use shredded oyster mushrooms.

BURRITOS DE DESHEBRADA

SHREDDED BEEF BRISKET BURRITOS

The north wouldn't be the same without *burritos*. A thin, homemade flour tortilla, rolled and filled with the tastiest stews is something that everyone loves. Every single northern state has its version and their own filling preference: Sonora is the state most famous for its incredible *burritos*. If you ever have the opportunity to visit this magical place, you need to try a *burrito percheron*, which is a *massive burrito* served using a 30cm tortilla. They are wrapped with a *tortilla sobaquera* (armpit tortilla), which get their name because they measure the length of an arm from the armpit.

This recipe is for the typical single filling *burrito* that you find on offer from a lot of street vendors. They only have one filling and are as thin as a flute, not like the massive burritos you see in some TexMex restaurants. Other common fillings are refried beans, potato with chorizo, shredded beef, *machaca*, *machaca* with scrambled eggs and *carne asada*.

MAKES 12

12 FLOUR TORTILLAS (SHOP-BOUGHT OR SEE PAGE 16 FOR HOMEMADE)

FOR THE BRISKET
350G BEEF BRISKET
2 BONE MARROW DISCS
½ ONION
2 GARLIC CLOVES
1 TBSP SEA SALT

FOR THE STEW
2 TBSP SUNFLOWER OIL
½ ONION, THINLY SLICED
2 GARLIC CLOVES, MINCED
½ ANAHEIM OR TURKISH 'YESIL TATLI BIBER' GREEN PEPPER, THINLY SLICED
3 PLUM TOMATOES, THINLY SLICED
1 TSP SEA SALT
COOKED BEEF BRISKET, SHREDDED (SEE ABOVE)
80ML BRISKET BROTH

TO SERVE
150G ICEBERG LETTUCE LEAVES
PICKLED JALAPEÑOS
JUST-FRIED PINTO BEANS (PAGE 45)

Make the flour tortillas the day before and keep them in the fridge, wrapped in a plastic zip-lock bag.

Preheat the oven to oven to 200°C (180°C fan/400°F/Gas 6).

Place the brisket in a cast-iron pot, add the bone marrow discs, onion, garlic, salt and 2 litres of water. Cover with a lid, place in the oven and cook for about 2 hours until the meat is very tender. Remove the pieces of brisket from the casserole and place on a plate to cool down; reserving the broth.

Once cooled, shred the brisket with either your hands or with the help of two forks, then chop it into small pieces. Set aside.

To start making the stew, heat the oil in a frying pan over a medium heat and add the onion and garlic. Fry for 2 minutes, then add the green pepper and continue frying for 4 minutes. Add the tomatoes and salt and continue frying until they have softened.

Once the vegetables are cooked, add the shredded brisket and brisket broth. Stir well, reduce the heat, cover with a lid and simmer for 10 minutes. Keep warm to serve.

Shred the lettuce and have the pickled jalapeños and fried beans ready, to construct the *burritos*.

Heat a frying pan to warm the homemade flour tortillas on both sides, then wrap them in a tea towel.

Grab a warm flour tortilla and place on a plate. Put some of the beef brisket stew in the middle and spread it downwards. Add a small amount of iceberg lettuce, then simply roll the tortilla up with two hands. You have youself the perfect northern-style *burrito*.

Serve together with some pickled jalapeños and fried pinto beans on the side.

MACHACA CON PAPAS

DRIED SHREDDED BEEF WITH POTATOES

In the essentials section (pages 14–35), you will find the recipe for making *machaca* from scratch. This recipe is one of the many ways we use the homemade *machaca* in the north of Mexico.

This dish is usually eaten for breakfast with some fried eggs on the side, fried pinto beans, and flour tortillas. A perfect way to start a day. I love cooking *machaca* at the weekends, when I have more time to cook and no one is in a hurry.

SERVES 4

3 TBSP VEGETABLE OIL

1 LARGE RED POTATO, PEELED AND CUT INTO 1CM DICE

½ ONION, FINELY CHOPPED

½ ANAHEIM OR TURKISH 'YESIL TATLI BIBER' GREEN PEPPER, OR GREEN BELL PEPPER, FINELY DICED

2 PLUM TOMATOES, FINELY DICED

150G MACHACA (PAGE 24)

TO SERVE

JUST-FRIED PINTO BEANS (PAGE 22)

FLOUR TORTILLAS (SHOP-BOUGHT OR SEE PAGE 16 FOR HOMEMADE)

SPICY SALSA

Heat the oil in a non-stick large frying pan over a medium heat and fry the potato for around 5 minutes, stirring constantly so that it is evenly cooked.

Add the onion and green pepper and fry for 3 minutes together with the potatoes, before adding the tomatoes. Fry for 2 more minutes.

Once all the vegetables are cooked and the potatoes are soft, add the *machaca* and fry for 3 minutes. Turn the heat off and serve with fried pinto beans on the side and warm flour tortillas.

CABRITO AL HORNO

OVEN-COOKED KID GOAT

Cabrito is a dish mostly cooked in the northeast states of Mexico – Coahuila, Tamaulipas, Durango and Nuevo León – where it is particularly popular among the locals. A *cabrito* is a young goat around 30 days old, still in the lactation stage and yet to start eating grass. When it is slaughtered, all the parts of the animal are used for cooking, with nothing going to waste.

The traditional method of cooking *cabrito* on a spit comes from the Sephardic Jewish community who founded Nuevo León around the 1500s, when they were expelled from Spain and arrived in Mexico alongside the Spanish explorers. Still the most common method to prepare a *cabrito* is by cutting open the kid goat, spearing with a metal rod, seasoning with salt and dried oregano, and roasting slowly over coal or mesquite wood. Another way of cooking *cabrito* is *al ataúd*, where the meat is placed in a metal box and wood and charcoal is lit over the top of the box, heating up the inside and roasting the meat.

The recipe here is for *cabrito al horno*, oven-cooked kid goat, which is another easier way to cook this meat. It's perfect for a Sunday family gathering. In London, you can buy kid goat at a butcher but, if you can't find it, you can always just use normal goat meat.

SERVES 4

1.2KG KID GOAT LEG

1 TSP SEA SALT

½ TSP GROUND BLACK PEPPER

1 TSP DRIED OREGANO

2 TBSP PORK LARD OR VEGETABLE OIL

TO SERVE

WARM CORN OR FLOUR TORTILLAS (SHOP-BOUGHT OR SEE PAGES 16 AND 18 FOR HOMEMADE)

SPICY SALSA OF YOUR CHOICE (PAGES 136–145)

JUST-FRIED PINTO BEANS (PAGE 45)

Preheat the oven to 200°C (180°C fan/400°F/Gas 6).

Place the kid goat leg on a baking tray and rub the salt and pepper all over, as well as the oregano and pork lard. Pour 250ml water into the tray and cover the tray with foil.

Cook in the oven for around 3 hours, or until the meat is tender and falling apart easily. Make sure to take it out a few times to baste the meat with cooking juices, so it does not dry out.

To serve, place on a platter, shredding some of the meat. People can add it to their own *tacos* with refried beans and spicy salsa.

GALLINA PINTA

PINTO BEANS, HOMINY & BEEF BROTH

This is a lovely broth from Sonora. The reasoning behind the name given to this dish is uncertain, but one of the versions says the *Gallina Pinta* (spotted hen) is so-called because of the way the *cacahuazintle* grains (pozole grains) look like a spotted hen, floating in the broth. It is one of the dishes that represents what Sonora is, as a lot of people make it at home. It is a comforting dish and super delicious. At home, I use pre-cooked pozole grains, that are easily available online. My children love adding all the toppings and squeezing lots of lime juice over it.

SERVES 4

6 PIECES OF OXTAIL

250G BEEF BRISKET, CUT INTO 5CM CUBES

1 ONION, PEELED AND HALVED

4 GARLIC CLOVES, PEELED

1 ANAHEIM OR TURKISH 'YESIL TATLI BIBER' GREEN PEPPER, OR GREEN BELL PEPPER

1 TSP DRIED OREGANO

1½ TBSP SEA SALT

500G COOKED PINTO BEANS, UNSALTED, KEEPING 200ML OF THE COOKING JUICE

500G PRE-COOKED HOMINY, RINSED

TO GARNISH

16G FRESH CORIANDER, FINELY CHOPPED

50G ONION, FINELY CHOPPED

8 *CHILTEPIN* CHILLIES, CRUSHED, OR 10G DRIED CHILLI FLAKES

2 LIMES, CUT INTO WEDGES

Place the oxtail pieces and brisket chunks in a large cast-iron pot. Add the onion, garlic, green pepper, oregano and salt. Pour over 2 litres of water and bring to the boil over a high heat. Remove any scum that forms on top and reduce the heat. Cover with a lid and simmer over a low heat for 1½ hours, or until the brisket is tender.

When the meat is tender, add the pre-cooked hominy and continue simmering over low heat for 15 minutes. Then add the cooked beans along with the bean cooking juice and cook for another 10 minutes. Turn the heat off and serve immediately.

Serve in bowls, garnished with fresh coriander, onion, crushed chilli or chilli flakes and a squeeze of lime juice.

CHILORIO

SHREDDED PORK IN ADOBO

Chilorio is a dish from the state of Sinaloa in north-west Mexico. This mouth-watering dish is packed with amazing flavours, made with pork meat cooked in water and lard. Then an *adobo* is made from the chillies and the pork is shredded and fried with this sauce, making it tender and a perfect filling for *burritos*, *tacos* or *tortas*. At home, I always have some *chilorio* in the freezer, as it is keeps very well.

SERVES 4

700G DICED PORK SHOULDER

½ ONION

5 GARLIC CLOVES, PEELED

3 BAY LEAVES

1 TSP SEA SALT

3 GUAJILLO CHILLIES

2 ANCHO CHILLIES

½ TSP DRIED OREGANO

½ TSP GROUND CUMIN

1 CLOVE

1 TBSP WHITE WINE VINEGAR

3 TBSP VEGETABLE OIL

TO SERVE

FLOUR OR CORN TORTILLAS (SHOP-BOUGHT OR SEE PAGES 16 AND 18 FOR HOMEMADE)

JUST-FRIED PINTO BEANS (PAGE 45)

FRESHLY CHOPPED CORIANDER

CHOPPED RED ONION

SPICY SALSA OF YOUR CHOICE (PAGES 136–145)

In a saucepan, add the pieces of pork with the onion, 2 garlic cloves, the bay leaves, 1 litre of water and salt. Bring to the boil, remove the scum that forms on top, then reduce the heat and simmer for 1 ½ hours until the meat is soft enough that it falls apart.

Meanwhile, put the guajillo and ancho chillies and 3 garlic cloves in a small pot, cover with water and bring to the boil. Reduce the heat and simmer for 10 minutes until the chillies are rehydrated.

Discard the water and place the rehydrated chillies in a blender together with the cooked garlic, oregano, spices and white wine vinegar. Blend until smooth, then pass the sauce through a sieve to remove any unwanted seeds or chilli peel. Set aside.

Heat the vegetable oil in a medium size cast-iron pot over medium heat and add the pieces of cooked pork meat, breaking them down until they look almost shredded. Add the chilli sauce and fry for 10 minutes. This is the *chilorio*.

Serve with some tortillas, refried beans, chopped coriander, onion and spicy salsa.

If the *chilorio* gets dry, add some of the pork stock left in the saucepan.

PUERCO EN CHILE COLORADO

PORK IN A RED CHILLI SAUCE

This is one of the dishes that originated during the viceroyalty. With the establishment of *haciendas* (estates) in northern Mexico, it gave way to gastronomic exchanges between *faeneros* (field workers) and *jornaleros* (day labourers), who were the employees working inside the *hacienda*.

The *chile colorado* chilli is the dried version of the Anaheim chilli, left to dry and mature into an intense red colour which we use to make a vibrant red sauce. It is kind of like a quick *mole* (the Nahuatl word for sauce), although it does not have as many ingredients as some of the *moles* of the south.

There are different versions made with beef, chicken or potatoes, but pork is the most popular. It is usually eaten for lunch on a weekday, as it does not take long to prepare. In my family, my mum loves cooking this dish with *nopalitos*, a tender edible cactus. It pairs really well with some nice red rice and flour tortillas.

SERVES 4

2 TBSP SUNFLOWER OIL

600G PORK SHOULDER STEAKS, CUT INTO 3CM CUBES

3 VINE TOMATOES, HALVED

½ ONION

4 GARLIC CLOVES, PEELED

1 TBSP SEA SALT

CHILE COLORADO SAUCE (PAGE 32)

TO SERVE

RED RICE (PAGE 56)

WARM CORN TORTILLAS (SHOP-BOUGHT OR SEE PAGE 18 FOR HOMEMADE)

Heat the sunflower oil in a cast-iron pot over a medium heat and add the pork pieces. Fry for 3–5 minutes, making sure to turn them to brown evenly. Once browned, add the tomatoes, onion, garlic, salt and 500ml water.

Bring to the boil and reduce the heat. Put the lid on and simmer for 1 hour until the pieces of pork are tender.

While the pork is cooking, make the chile colorado sauce (page 32). When the pork is cooked, pour the chile colorado sauce over it. Simmer over a low heat for 15 minutes.

Serve with some red rice and warm corn tortillas.

DOGOS ESTILO SONORA

MEXICAN HOT DOGS

MAKES 10

10 LONG SLICES OF DRY-
  CURED STREAKY BACON
10 FRANKFURTER SAUSAGES
1 TBSP VEGETABLE OIL
450ML HOT WATER
10 AMERICAN HOT DOG
  BUNS, SLICED SIDEWAYS

FOR THE FRIED ONION
2 TBSP BUTTER
1 TBSP VEGETABLE OIL
1 ONION, THINLY SLICED

**FOR THE TOMATO AND
ONION SALSA**
2 PLUM TOMATOES, FINELY
  CHOPPED
¼ ONION, FINELY CHOPPED
½ TSP SEA SALT

FOR THE TOPPINGS
1 LARGE GHERKIN, FINELY
  DICED
3 WHOLE PICKLED
  JALAPEÑOS, FINELY
  CHOPPED
1 BAG OF READY SALTED
  CRISPS, CRUSHED
MAYONNAISE
AMERICAN MUSTARD
KETCHUP

You are probably wondering why there is an American recipe in this book, but let me tell you that hot dogs are something that we love eating in the north of Mexico. I would say that they are almost as popular as *tacos*.

Sonora is very famous for the amazing ways of serving a hot dog; they call them *dogos*. There are a few differences between an American and a Mexican hot dog. In Mexico, the buns are steamed, the Frankfurter sausages are wrapped in bacon and fried and there is always some sort of spicy salsa or pickled jalapeños that will be added.

The sky is the limit when it comes to garnishing a hot dog in Sonora, as they have a lot of different toppings from the simplest one to the more complex (fried onion, crushed salted crisps, guacamole, spicy salsas, melted cheese, etc). You are free to make your own concoction and add as many as you can handle. Vegans and vegetarians, use plant-based options in place of the bacon and Frankfurters.

Start by melting the butter over a medium heat, adding the oil to stop the butter burning. Add the sliced onion, then reduce the heat and gently fry for 10 minutes. Turn off the heat and set the onions aside for later use.

To make the tomato and onion salsa, mix the tomatoes and onion together. Add the salt and set aside.

Put the topping ingredients in separate bowls. Set the bowls aside for later use, ready for people to help themselves.

Wrap a piece of bacon tightly around each sausage.

In a frying pan, heat the oil and fry the sausages over a medium heat for around 5 minutes until the bacon is fried. Set aside.

Line a metal steamer with greaseproof paper to stop the buns sticking.

Pour the hot water into a saucepan and place the metal steamer over the top. Place the buns in the metal steamer and cover with a lid. They will become soft in a few minutes. You might have to do this in batches.

To make the perfect *dogo*, open a steamed hot dog bun, spread over some mayo and place the sausage in. Coat with ketchup and mustard and finish with a little of every topping. Enjoy as many as you can eat!

SOPES SINALOENSES

SHREDDED BEEF & POTATO CORN PATTIES

Sopes are little round corn dough patties that are cooked and then fried; stuffed with many different things depending on the region of Mexico you are in. I usually add a simple topping, like refried beans. But when I feel like preparing a treat, I make *sopes sinaloenses* (Sinaloa-style *sopes*), which are topped with mashed potato mixed with shredded beef and garnished with lots of different things: fresh vegetables, pickled red onion, soured cream, cheese and the most exquisite beef broth, made from cooking the beef for hours.

When we make *sopes* at home, we make plenty. My mum usually cooks the meat a day in advance to save time. My sister Cynthia makes the dough, I chop all the veggies, and we all help to serve them. It is one of the dishes that, every time I make them, really takes me back to memories of my mum's or grandma's house.

MAKES 16

FOR THE FILLING
150G BEEF BRISKET

3 BONE MARROW DISCS

2 PLUM TOMATOES, HALVED

½ ONION, PEELED

2 GARLIC CLOVES, PEELED

1½ TBSP SEA SALT

2 MEDIUM RED POTATOES, COOKED, PEELED AND MASHED

1 TBSP TOMATO PURÉE

½ TSP DRIED OREGANO

FOR THE SOPES
300G MASA HARINA (GMO-FREE CORN FLOUR)

1 TSP GARLIC SALT

¼ WHITE ONION, GRATED

450ML WARM WATER

450ML SUNFLOWER OIL

TO GARNISH
2 HANDFULS OF ICEBERG LETTUCE, FINELY SHREDDED

2 SMALL CARROTS, PEELED AND GRATED

7 RADISHES, THINLY SLICED

½ CUCUMBER, PEELED, DESEEDED AND CUT INTO THIN HALF-MOONS

1 PERFECTLY RIPE HASS AVOCADO, PEELED AND THINLY SLICED

180G *QUESO FRESCO* OR FETA CHEESE, CRUMBLED

120ML SOURED CREAM, MIXED WITH 1 TBSP MILK TO MAKE IT RUNNY

30G PICKLED RED ONION (PAGE 29)

SPICY SALSA OF YOUR CHOICE (PAGES 136–145) (OPTIONAL)

Continues overleaf

Preheat the oven to 200°C (180°C fan/400°F/Gas 6).

Put the brisket, bone marrow, tomatoes, onion, garlic, 1 tablespoon of salt and 2 litres of water in a cast-iron pot and cook in the oven for 2 hours until the meat is very tender and falls apart easily. Alternatively, the brisket can be cooked on the hob. This gives you more control as it's easier to check if the brisket is running out of water. If cooking on the hob, cook the brisket over a low heat for about 2 hours.

Remove the brisket from the pot and leave to cool. Shred the meat into thin strips then chop into small pieces. Mix with the mashed potato and ½ teaspoon of salt. Set aside.

Remove the tomatoes, onion and garlic cloves from the pot and blend until smooth. Pour this sauce back into the broth, then add tomato purée and oregano and remove the pieces of bone marrow. Bring the broth to the boil, turn off the heat and set aside.

To make the sopes, place the flour in a large bowl, add the garlic salt and grated onion. Gradually add the water and 100ml of the warm brisket broth little by little. Mix until it has formed a moist dough.

Heat a large pan over a medium heat and make 16 dough balls, weighing 50g each. Form each dough ball into a patty around 10cm in diameter and 3mm thick. Put each patty on the hot pan and cook on one side for 30 seconds, then, with the help of a spatula, flip it over. Cook on the other side until firm, for about 1½ minutes, then flip over again. Each patty takes around 5 minutes to cook.

Once cooked, remove the patties from the pan and leave them to cool on a wire rack. With your hands, pinch the edges of each patty upwards to form a rim. Set aside.

In a frying pan, heat the sunflower oil over a medium heat. Fry the sopes in batches for 1 minute on each side. Remove the sopes with the help of some kitchen tongs and place on kitchen paper to absorb any excess oil.

To serve, place the sopes on a large serving plate and top each one with the beef and potato filling, then some of each garnish to finish. Add some salsa if you want some heat. You can either serve the broth in a separate cup, add some broth to each sope, or pour the broth over them all at once.

MENUDO BLANCO

WHITE TRIPE & HOMINY SOUP

In Mexico, *menudo* (tripe), also known as *pancita* (little stomach), is a soup made with cow's stomach that is one of those dishes that people either love or hate. It is usually made in big batches for special occasions like weddings, birthdays or social gatherings – and is widely believed to be a great hangover cure. Guests are invited back again the next day to cure their hangovers with a bowl of leftover homemade *menudo*.

In my family, my parents always cook *menudo* on Christmas Eve (the most important day for Mexicans to celebrate Christmas). We don't eat it that day, but we prepare it for breakfast on the 25th when everyone is tired and has had a little bit too much to drink.

This is a traditional recipe that supposedly came about due to availability and necessity. The stomach was a part of the cow not used by affluent Spaniards, and the butchers didn't want to sell good cuts of meat to the indigenous people. Therefore, they started to sell unwanted and other unused parts of the cow to the so-called lower classes. The recipe has suffered from squeamish scrutiny in recent years but is regaining popularity to secure its place as one of the favourite celebration recipes in the north.

In the north, this soup is usually made with cow's tripe, beef or pig's trotters and hominy; flavoured with onion, garlic and a popular green chilli used in a lot of northern recipes. In the states of Sinaloa, Sonora, Baja California and Baja California Sur, the broth is usually white and in Chihuahua and Nuevo León it's red, because of the addition of blended guajillo chillies. Here in London, I usually buy my tripe at an Iranian butchers, where it is sold cleaned and ready to cook.

SERVES 4

650G TRIPE, CLEANED AND CUT INTO 3CM SQUARES
2 BONE MARROW DISCS
½ TSP DRIED OREGANO
½ ONION, PEELED
1 GREEN BELL PEPPER, STEM REMOVED AND DESEEDED
5 GARLIC CLOVES, PEELED
1 TBSP SEA SALT
400G PRE-COOKED HOMINY, DRAINED AND RINSED

TO SERVE

1 SMALL ONION, FINELY CHOPPED
SMALL BUNCH OF FRESH CORIANDER, FINELY CHOPPED
10 FRESH RADISHES, THINLY SLICED
DRIED OREGANO
2 LIMES, CUT INTO WEDGES
CRUSHED *CHILTEPIN* CHILLIES OR DRIED CHILLI FLAKES
1 BAGUETTE, SLICED

Put the tripe in a large saucepan. Add the bone marrow discs, oregano, onion, green pepper, garlic cloves, salt and 2 litres of water. Bring to the boil over a high heat, removing any scum that forms on the surface. Reduce the heat and simmer for 1½ hours, making sure to remove the fat that forms on the top from time to time.

Add the pre-cooked hominy and cook for a further 30 minutes, or until the maize is soft.

To serve, add some pieces of tripe into bowls with some hominy and broth, garnish with onion and coriander, radishes, a pinch of dried oregano, a squeeze of lime juice and some crushed *chiltepin*. Use the baguette to soak up any juices.

WAKABAKI

BEEF & VEGETABLE BROTH

The word *wakabaki* is a Mayo word that means 'cow broth'. The dish is a traditional nutritious beef broth cooked in the states of Sonora and Sinaloa. The indigenous Yaqui tribe cook *wakabaki* for very special occasions, like weddings, funerals or town festivities. The beef is cooked for a few hours until tender, using bone marrow to make it substantial, and then seasonal vegetables are added, like cabbage, carrots and corn on the cob.

Even though this is a festive dish, my dad used to make *wakabaki* all year round, even during the hot summer months. A big batch of *wakabaki* will provide leftovers that can last you many mealtimes.

SERVES 4

600G BEEF SHIN WITH BONE MARROW, OR STEWING STEAK

2 BONE MARROW DISCS

1 ONION, PEELED AND HALVED

3 PLUM TOMATOES, HALVED

4 GARLIC CLOVES, PEELED

1 TBSP SEA SALT

15 BABY POTATOES

6 CARROTS, PEELED AND CUT INTO CHUNKS

2 CORN ON THE COB, CUT INTO 8 DISCS

240G COOKED CHICKPEAS, DRAINED

1 SMALL WHITE CABBAGE, CUT INTO 4 WEDGES

4 SMALL COURGETTES, CUT INTO CHUNKS

20 GREEN BEANS

TO SERVE

CRUSHED *CHILTEPIN* CHILLI OR DREID CHILLI FLAKES

1 LIME, CUT INTO WEDGES

WARM CORN TORTILLAS (SHOP-BOUGHT OR SEE PAGE 18 FOR HOMEMADE)

AVOCADO SLICES

Put the meat, bone marrow discs, onion, tomatoes, garlic, salt and 1.75 litres of water in a large cast-iron pot. Bring to the boil over a medium heat and remove the scum that forms on the top. Reduce the heat and simmer for 1½ hours.

Add the baby potatoes, carrots and corn and cook for 10 minutes. Then add the chickpeas and white cabbage and continue to simmer for 5 minutes. Add the courgettes and green beans and cook for a further 10 minutes.

The *wakabaki* is ready when all the vegetables are tender and the meat is falling apart easily.

Serve in bowls. Add some pieces of meat and a few of each vegetable. Scatter with crushed chilli and squeeze over some lime juice. Grab a tortilla and add some avocado slices, roll it up like a *taco* and eat with the *wakabaki*.

CAZUELA DE MACHACA

DRIED BEEF SOUP

Cazuela de Machaca is one of the many dishes where *machaca*, dried meat, is used. This soup is particularly popular in Sonora, Chihuahua and Sinaloa. *Machaca* is one of the ingredients most widely used in the north of Mexico. At home, my dad used to make this soup on a rainy day. It is comforting and easy to make when you are in a hurry.

SERVES 4

3 TBSP VEGETABLE OIL

2 LARGE RED POTATOES, PEELED AND CUT INTO 3CM CUBES

1 SMALL ONION, FINELY CHOPPED

2 GARLIC CLOVES, MINCED

2 ANAHEIM OR CARLISTON TURKISH GREEN PEPPERS, CHARRED, PEELED, DESEEDED AND CUT INTO LONG STRIPS (PAGE 26)

3 PLUM TOMATOES, GRATED

150G MACHACA (PAGE 24)

1 TSP SEA SALT

WARM FLOUR OR CORN TORTILLAS, TO SERVE (SHOP-BOUGHT OR SEE PAGES 16 AND 18 FOR HOMEMADE)

In a saucepan, heat the oil over a medium heat and add the potatoes. Fry for 3 minutes, stirring constantly. Add the onion and garlic and continue frying for another 3 minutes.

Then add the pepper strips, followed by the grated tomatoes and fry for 3 minutes on a medium heat before adding the *machaca*, salt and 1.5 litres of water. Reduce the heat and cover with a lid. Simmer for 10 minutes, or until the potatoes are soft.

Serve in bowls with warm flour or corn tortillas.

POLLO A LAS BRASAS ESTILO SINALOA

SINALOA-STYLE GRILLED CHICKEN

In Sinaloa, there is a famous restaurant chain call 'El Pollo Loco' (crazy chicken) that grills chicken. I would dare to say that it is almost an institution, as it has been in business since 1975, the company has even crossed the border and has restaurants in the USA as well. Inspired by this, you can now find a lot of other restaurants making this grilled-style chicken, marinated with spices and orange.

At home, I love making this recipe on a Sunday because it is perfect for sharing with the family; everyone helps themselves and makes their own *tacos*. I buy frozen fries, to cook in the oven and pile on as a cheeky addition to our *tacos*, just like they do in the restaurants in Mexico.

SERVES 4

1 WHOLE CHICKEN, APPROX. 1.5KG, BUTTERFLIED (ASK YOUR BUTCHER TO DO THIS FOR YOU)

FOR THE MARINADE
5 GARLIC CLOVES, MINCED
JUICE OF 1 ORANGE
JUICE OF 2 LIMES
80G PAPAYA OR PINEAPPLE
2 TBSP AMERICAN MUSTARD
1 TSP DRIED OREGANO
4 BLACK PEPPERCORNS
1 TBSP SEA SALT

FOR THE TOMATO SALSA
3 PLUM TOMATOES
¼ ONION
3 JALAPEÑOS
PINCH OF SEA SALT
JUICE OF ½ LIME

TO SERVE
15 WARM CORN TORTILLAS (SHOP-BOUGHT OR SEE PAGE 18 FOR HOMEMADE)
FROZEN FRIES (OPTIONAL)

In a blender, add the garlic, orange and lime juice, papaya, mustard, oregano, peppercorns, salt and 120ml water. Blend until smooth.

Put the whole chicken in a large plastic bag or bowl and pour in the marinade, rubbing it in all over. Leave to marinate in the fridge for at least 2 hours or overnight.

Once the chicken is marinated, take it out of the fridge an hour before cooking, to reach room temperature.

Light the barbecue. Place the coals in the middle of the crate until they glow white, then spread them onto one side.

Put the chicken, skin-side up, on the side of the barbecue with no coals underneath, close the barbecue lid and cook for 40 minutes. Next open the barbecue and carefully flip the chicken to grill on the other side for 20 minutes. Then place the chicken directly over the charcoal for 15 minutes, making sure it does not burn, which will give a smoky flavour.

While the chicken is cooking, make the tomato salsa. Put the tomatoes, onion, jalapeños, salt, lime juice and 5 tablespoons water in a food processor and blitz until all the ingredients are in little pieces. Set aside.

By this point the chicken should be cooked. To test, place a temperature probe into the thickest part of the chicken. If it shows 70°C (158°F), then it is properly cooked. If you do not have a probe, insert a knife in the side of the chicken leg and if the juices run clear, it is cooked.

Warm the tortillas and cook some fries according to the packet instructions, if you like.

Remove the chicken from the barbecue and cut into pieces. Serve on a platter with the tomato salsa, corn tortillas and fries. People can help themselves to make their own *tacos*.

Alternatively, cook in the oven. Place the chicken on a baking tray in a preheated oven at 200°C (180°C fan/400°F/Gas 6). Roast the chicken for 1 hour and 20 minutes or until the juices are running clear.

FRIJOLES CHARROS

CHARRO BEANS

This is an old recipe from the north of Mexico, usually made by the *charros* (cowboys), who were in charge of looking after animals in the fields. They would cook the beans with whatever additions they had; usually adding preserved meats like chorizo, plus herbs and chillies for flavour variation. Nowadays, it is common to see this dish cooked in households instead of ranches. This is one of my favourite ways to cook beans, as the accompanying ingredients are easy to find in shops.

SERVES 4

2 TBSP SUNFLOWER OIL

½ ONION, FINELY CHOPPED

1 LARGE GARLIC CLOVE, FINELY CHOPPED

7 STREAKY BACON RASHERS, CHOPPED

70G VEGAN CHORIZO (PAGE 44 FOR HOMEMADE)

6 COOKED HAM SLICES, CHOPPED (OPTIONAL)

½ ANAHEIM, TURKISH 'YESIL TATLI BIBER' GREEN PEPPER OR GREEN BELL PEPPER, CHARRED, STEM REMOVED, DESEEDED AND DICED (PAGE 26)

2 TOMATOES, DICED

1 TSP SEA SALT

800G COOKED PINTO BEANS WITH THEIR COOKING JUICE (PAGE 22)

400ML HOT WATER

CHOPPED FRESH CORIANDER, TO SERVE (OPTIONAL)

Heat the oil in a large saucepan over a medium heat. Add the onion and garlic and fry for 2 minutes, stirring constantly to avoid burning. Add the chopped streaky bacon and fry for 3 minutes.

Once the bacon is semi-cooked, add the vegan chorizo and ham, if using. Fry on a low heat for 5 minutes. Then add the green pepper and tomatoes. Cook for another 3 minutes. Season with the salt.

Add the pinto beans with their cooking juice plus the hot water. Mix and put the lid on to bring to the boil. Reduce the heat to low and simmer for 10 minutes.

Serve in bowls, topped with some chopped coriander.

NACHOS

Despite a lot of people thinking that nachos are a TexMex creation, *nachos* are originally from from Piedras Negras, a north Mexican town in Coahuila, where they hold a festival every year to celebrate this iconic dish.

In Mexico, the nickname for a person called Ignacio is 'Nacho'; a shorter version of the name. Legend says that there was a restaurant in the city, owned by Ignacio Anaya. One day a group of American ladies arrived and ordered some food. That particular day, he didn't have much to serve, so he placed some tortilla chips on a plate, added some local cheese on top, which he then melted in the oven and scattered over some pickled jalapeños. He served this to the hungry ladies, who loved the dish and kept coming back to eat Nacho's special, which was soon named after him. It quickly became a popular dish, not only in America, but all around the world. Over the years, the recipe has evolved from just simple melted cheese and pickled jalapeños, to nowadays being served with cheese sauce and extra toppings like guacamole, *salsa bandera*, beans, olives and steak strips.

I love making *nachos* at home, but it is difficult to find the right gooey cheese similar to the one we get in Mexico, so I make my own nacho cheese version.

SERVES 4

100G BAVETTE STEAK, CUT IN THINLY STRIPS, COOKED TO YOUR LIKING

200G BAG OF GOOD-QUALITY *TOTOPOS* (TORTILLA CHIPS)

240G *SALSA BANDERA* (PAGE 28)

1 PERFECTLY RIPE HASS AVOCADO, MASHED

90G BLACK OLIVES, THINLY SLICED

SLICED PICKLED JALAPEÑOS

FOR THE CHEESE SAUCE

1 TBSP CORNFLOUR

200ML COLD WHOLE MILK

20G BUTTER

50G RED LEICESTER, GRATED

50G CHEDDAR CHEESE, GRATED

1 TBSP PICKLED JALAPEÑO VINEGAR

1 TSP SEA SALT

OTHER OPTIONAL TOPPINGS

COOKED PINTO BEANS

SOURED CREAM

Start by making the cheese sauce. Dissolve the cornflour in the cold milk. Set aside.

In a saucepan, melt the butter over a medium heat and add the milk and cornflour mixture.

Using a mini metal whisk, whisk the mixture until it begins to bubble. As soon as the consistency has thickened, turn off the heat and add the grated cheeses, vinegar and salt. Mix until the cheeses have melted and the cheese sauce is runny.

To make the nachos, first grill the steak strips to your liking. Place the tortilla chips on a plate, pour the cheese sauce over the top and scatter with some *salsa bandera*, mashed avocado, sliced olives, pickled jalapeños and the steak strips.

Enjoy with friends and some nice Frozen Margaritas (page 164).

For a vegetarian alternative, simply omit the steak.

GORDITAS DE PICADILLO

MINCED BEEF CORN PATTIES

Gorditas are one of the most popular street foods sold in Mexico. They are little round pockets made with corn or wheat dough and stuffed with different fillings.

In Coahuila, Durango and Chihuahua, they are made using wheat flour. I like to make them with masa harina, because this is the way we make them in my family. My favourite filling is *picadillo*, something that I make not only for stuffing *gorditas*, but also to put on top of a *sope* (corn patty, page 118) or serve by itself with some rice and refried beans. This is perfect for a delicious lunch or dinner.

MAKES 10

300G MASA HARINA (GMO-FREE CORN FLOUR)
½ TSP GARLIC SALT
500ML WARM WATER

FOR THE PICADILLO
2 TBSP VEGETABLE OIL
½ ONION, FINELY CHOPPED
2 GARLIC CLOVES, MINCED
200G MINCED BEEF
3 PLUM TOMATOES, FINELY CHOPPED
½ ANAHEIM, TURKISH 'YESIL TATLI BIBER' GREEN PEPPER, OR GREEN BELL PEPPER
1 LARGE CARROT, PEELED AND FINELY DICED
1 LARGE POTATO, PEELED AND FINELY DICED
1 TSP SEA SALT
PINCH OF GROUND BLACK PEPPER

TO SERVE
SOURED CREAM
CRUMBLED *QUESO FRESCO* OR FETA CHEESE
SPICY SALSA OF YOUR CHOICE (PAGES 136–145)

Start by making the *picadillo*. Heat the oil in a large frying pan over a medium heat. Add the onion and garlic and fry for 2 minutes. When the onion is translucent, add the minced beef and cook until browned, making sure to break it down.

Add the tomatoes, green pepper, diced carrots and potatoes. Season with the salt and pepper. Add a splash of water, cover with a lid, reduce the heat to low and simmer for 20 minutes. Set aside.

Move on to make the *gorditas*, In a large bowl, add the masa harina, garlic salt and warm water. Mix well until the flour has absorbed the water.

Heat a large non-stick frying pan over a medium heat.

Separate the dough into 70g balls and, using a tortilla press, flatten them into 3mm-thick discs.

Cook the *gorditas* in the frying pan for 1 minute, then flip over. Cook for around 4 minutes.

Once the *gordita* is cooked, remove it from the heat. With the help of a knife, open it carefully by slicing through the edge, making a little pocket.

Fill it with *picadillo* and add some soured cream, cheese and spicy salsa.

CARNE ASADA

NORTHERN-STYLE BBQ

In the north of Mexico, *carne asada* means much more than a steak taco with guacamole and spicy salsa. A *carne asada* is a well-orchestrated event, something that us northerners do on the weekends to chill out with friends and forget about our problems. We grow up playing around the grill, breathing in the smoky aromas, watching the grown-ups flipping steaks. It's in our blood.

Eating a *carne asada taco* standing in a *taqueria* (a place to eat tacos) is one of the best things that one can experience. Watching the master *taquero* (the person who makes the *tacos* in a *taqueria*) making an *asada taco* is like watching a juggling show. It is incredible to see his skills in manoeuvring a knife, almost as big as a machete, when chopping the steaks into small pieces. He then grabs a corn tortilla and fills it with grilled meat, quickly scooping in a mixture of chopped onion and fresh coriander and magically mixing in one hand. He finishes the *taco* with a vibrant red spicy salsa which is thrown into the air and lands on top of the *taco*. All this happens in a matter of seconds. I have never understood how he manages to do it!

But we also love making *asada tacos* at home. A *carne asada* means to have a party with family and celebrate good times the best way we know how – with food. The grill is an important part of any Mexican household; most own one in their backyards as an extension of the kitchen. In my family, we have a brick one that has sat there for many years. It is now part of our family – if our grill could talk, it would tell amazing stories of great gatherings of eating, drinking and music. My dad was always trying to find an excuse to throw a *carne asada* and he always succeeded, so every weekend the *asador* (grill) would be fired up and we would all contribute by making the side dishes.

If you ever get invited to a *carne asada*, be prepared to get blown away and eat a lot – it is probably the most memorable Mexican event that you will ever experience. For northerners, a *carne asada* is our way of showing we like you, we care for you and we want to celebrate life with you. In other words, *carne asada* is love.

Arriba el norte!

A *carne asada* table is full of lots of different dishes, try out a couple of my menu plan spreads next time you plan a feast for friends or family:

MENU 1

BAVETTE STEAK WITH VEGETABLES (PAGE 99)
NACHOS (PAGE 127)
FLOUR TORTILLAS (PAGE 16)
PINTO BEANS FROM THE POT (PAGE 22)
CHARRED CHILLIES & SPRING ONIONS (PAGE 31)
GUACAMOLE (PAGE 27)
TOMATO, ONION & JALAPEÑO SALSA (PAGE 28)
FRESH RADISHES
CHOPPED FRESH ONION & CORIANDER
LIME WEDGES
CUCUMBER & LIME WATER (PAGE 171)
TOMATO JUICE & BEER (PAGE 166)
MEXICAN FLAN (PAGE 150)

MENU 2

COURGETTES WITH CHEESE (PAGE 50)
VEGAN CHORIZO WITH POTATOES (PAGE 44)
MEXICAN CACTUS SALAD (PAGE 52)
CORN TORTILLAS (PAGE 18)
JUST–FRIED PINTO BEANS (PAGE 45)
PICKLED RED ONION (PAGE 29)
LIME WEDGES
GUACAMOLE (PAGE 27)
CREAMY RED SALSA (PAGE 144)
CHIA & LIME WATER (PAGE 170)
FROZEN MARGARITAS (PAGE 164)
MANGO, LIME & CHILLI ICE LOLLIES
(PAGE 159)

ALGO
PICOSITO

SOMETHING SPICY

Chillies are a fundamental part of Mexican cuisine; a symbol of identity which plays a main role in lots of our dishes. The sixty-four types of domesticated chillies and more than 200 criollo species have been in the Mexican diet for a long time.

In the north of Mexico, the most popular chilli is the *chiltepin* – 'red gold', as people call it, as it is one of the most expensive chillies in Mexico because it is difficult to grow and harvest. These little round red gems are the crown jewels for a lot of northern recipes, with their fruity aroma and high level of heat, they are perfect in a *taco de carne asada* (steak taco) or a *machaca* (dried meat) stew or broth.

Another chilli, well-known among northerners, is the Anaheim pepper or *chile verde*; a long, thin green pepper, not spicy, but added to a lot of stews for flavour. When it is dried it is called *chile colorado,* or red chilli. A dried chilli that's widely used in Durando and Chihuhua is the *chile pasado*, which is dried differently to *chile colorado*. The *chile pasado* is a poblano chilli that first is charred, then left to dry completely under the sun, while the *chile colorado* is an Anaheim chilli that is sun-dried only.

Since I moved to London, I'm used to hearing things like, 'you're Mexican, you must be able to handle spicy food!' or questions like 'is all Mexican food spicy?'. The answer is: no, to both things. I love spicy food, but I consider myself a Mexican with an average tolerance to medium heat. Not all Mexican food is spicy, but what *are* spicy are our salsas.

No Mexican meal can be enjoyed without a good, fiery, spicy salsa. At home, my dad always made sure we had a freshly made one every time we sat down to eat. He was in complete and utter love with his *molcajete* (pestle and mortar), with which he would make magic. He loved experimenting and, like an alchemist, he would make wonderful and delicious chilli combinations.

Any Mexican would agree that a good *taco* or a delicious Mexican breakfast, is not complete without its spicy partner, the *salcita*. They're just not the same without a proper amount of heat, and salsas can complement many other dishes, too. I've collected my favourite salsa recipes, one or two are from the north and others are popular around all Mexico. Just a spoonful is enough to elevate any of the dishes in this book.

SALSA TATEMADA
CHARRED SALSA

This is my favourite salsa because it was my dad's favourite. Every time he would make this spicy salsa, we'd have to leave the house, as the chilli fumes would get into every corner and make us cough. I have fond memories of him toasting the chillies and grinding them in his beloved *molcajete* (Mexican stone mortar), then he would make himself some salsa *tacos*.

This is one of the most common salsas that people make all around Mexico, and a wonderful spicy salsa to have on the table to add into everything. I don't use as many chillies as my dad used to, so it is well balanced. Just remember to open the windows when toasting the chillies to prevent having a spicy rush to your head!

SERVES 4

2 SMALL GARLIC CLOVES, UNPEELED

40G ONION, PEELED AND WHOLE

2 PLUM TOMATOES

15 DRIED ARBOL CHILLIES, STEMS REMOVED

120ML HOT WATER

½ TSP SEA SALT

JUICE OF 1 LIME

Heat a comal (Mexican flat griddle pan) or a dry frying pan over high heat. Place the garlic cloves, onion and plum tomatoes into the hot pan, there's no need to add any oil. Char them until the skin is black. Remember to remove the garlic as soon as it turns black and remove its skin, setting the peeled cloves aside.

Toast the arbol chillies for no longer than a minute, tossing them around so they do not burn. This will enhance the flavour. Take them out of the pan and place in the hot water for 10 minutes to soften. Remove the chillies and reserve the chilli water for later use. Roughly chop the chillies and set aside.

There are two ways to make this salsa: in a *molcajete* (pestle and mortar) or in a blender.

If using a *molcajete*, start by mashing the garlic, adding the salt.

Finely chop the charred onion, then add it to the *molcajete* and mash until puréed. Add the arbol chillies, mashing them with the pestle as much as you can. Add the tomatoes and mash until it becomes a paste. Adjust the consistency with the addition of some reserved chilli water to make it runny. Squeeze in the lime juice. Leave in the *molcajete* to serve.

If using a blender, add the charred garlic, onion, tomatoes, rehydrated arbol chillies and salt to a blender, adding a quarter of the reserved water. Blend until smooth. Pour into a bowl and let it set before adding the lime juice and more reserved chilli water if the consistency is too thick.

SALSA MACHA

OIL-BASED SALSA

The first time I tried *salsa macha* was in Ensenada, I didn't know what it was, but I quickly got addicted to it. I love the fact that it can be kept in the cupboard for many months, as it is an oil-based salsa. It's a delicious and super spicy salsa that goes with everything, including eggs, soups, *tacos* or broths. In the north of Mexico, you will always find this salsa over *tacos* or *antojitos*. This particular recipe goes well with peanuts, but simply omit if you are making this recipe for someone who is intolerant.

MAKES APPROX. 350G

350G SUNFLOWER OIL

¼ ONION, PEELED, CUT INTO 3CM CHUNKS

2 GARLIC CLOVES, PEELED

30 ARBOL CHILLIES, STEMS REMOVED

30G SESAME SEEDS

1 TSP SEA SALT

20G BLANCHED PEANUTS, ROUGHLY CHOPPED (OPTIONAL)

In a small saucepan, heat the oil over a medium heat. Once hot, reduce the heat and add the onion. Fry for about 3 minutes, making sure it does not burn or get too brown. Then add the garlic cloves and fry for 2 minutes.

Add the arbol chillies, mix well and fry for another 3 minutes. Don't let them turn black, otherwise the salsa will taste bitter.

Now add half of the sesame seeds and the salt. Fry all the ingredients together over a very low heat for 3 minutes, stirring from time to time to stop the chillies from burning. Turn off the heat and leave the oil and chillies to cool completely.

Once cool, add everything into a blender and blitz until the chillies are broken down into little pieces.

Return the *salsa macha* to the saucepan and add the remaining sesame seeds and peanuts, mixing well. The texture of the *salsa macha* needs to be a bit chunky, with some chilli seeds still visible.

Store in a sterilized jar in the cupboard for up to 6 months.

GUACASALSA

SPICY AVOCADO SALSA

This is an easy and quick salsa to make for when you are having *tacos*. It is quite popular among Mexicans, especially in *taquerias* (a street food place that sells tacos). The ingredients are easily available in any supermarket. These days, there are a lot of supermarkets where you can find fresh jalapeños, but if you can't find them, use any spicy green chillies that are available.

SERVES 4

1 PERFECTLY RIPE HASS AVOCADO

2 SPRING ONIONS, ROUGHLY CHOPPED

1–2 JALAPEÑOS, ROUGHLY CHOPPED

1 SMALL GARLIC CLOVE, ROUGHLY CHOPPED

½ TSP SEA SALT

JUICE OF ½ LIME

5 SPRIGS OF FRESH CORIANDER

Cut the avocado in half and, using a spoon, scoop out the flesh and place it into a blender. Add the spring onions, jalapeños, garlic, salt, lime juice, 100ml water and coriander. Blend until it is a loose, smooth consistency.

Serve in a bowl and pour onto any *taco* of your choice.

SALSA VERDE

TOMATILLO SALSA

This is a crowd-pleasing salsa loved all over Mexico, not just in the north. It goes really well with *tacos*; especially fish or steak. I prefer using fresh tomatillos when I make this salsa, as they are less sour and, these days, it is easy to source them in the UK, online or sometimes in greengrocers. If you can't find fresh, used canned ones as they are a good alternative and are ready to use once drained.

MAKES APPROX. 350G

5 FRESH TOMATILLOS, PEELED AND WASHED

50G ONION, PEELED

3 FRESH JALAPEÑOS, STEM REMOVED

1 GARLIC CLOVE, PEELED

1 TBSP SEA SALT

2 TBSP FRESH CORIANDER, ROUGHLY CHOPPED

There are two methods to make this recipe: cooked or charred.

FOR THE COOKED METHOD

Add the tomatillos, onion, jalapeños and garlic to a saucepan, along with 500ml water.

Bring to the boil, then reduce the heat to low. Simmer for 10 minutes. Remove the vegetables from the saucepan, reserving the water for later use.

Place the vegetables into a blender, add the coriander and salt, and blitz until smooth.

FOR THE CHARRED METHOD

Heat a frying pan over high heat and place the tomatillos, onion, jalapeños and garlic until charred. Make sure to remove the garlic as soon as its skin is black. Remove the vegetables from the pan and leave them to cool to room temperature.

Put the vegetables in a blender, add the coriander and salt, and blitz until smooth. Alternatively, mash the vegetables in a *molcajete* or pestle and mortar, following the same method as the charred salsa.

Add some water, if the consistency is too thick. Serve and enjoy over some tacos.

Keep in the fridge for up to 3 days.

SALSA TAQUERA

CREAMY RED SALSA

This delicious salsa is always found in a good *taqueria* (a street food place that sells tacos). It is very easy to make and has a creamy texture that complements any flavour combination of *taco*. Just like the rest of the salsas, this one can be made in advance of a dinner party or meal, and can be kept in the fridge for up to 5 days.

MAKES APPROX. 180ML

80ML VEGETABLE OIL

¼ SMALL ONION, CUT INTO MEDIUM CHUNKS

2 TOMATOES, CUT INTO MEDIUM CHUNKS

1 GARLIC CLOVE, PEELED

12 ARBOL CHILLIES, STEMS REMOVED

1 TSP SEA SALT

In a small frying pan, heat half the oil over a medium heat and add the onion. Fry for 2 minutes until translucent.

Next add the tomatoes, garlic and arbol chillies. Fry everything together for around 3 minutes. Remove from the heat and leave to cool to room temperature.

Place all the ingredients in a blender, then add the salt and the remaining oil. Blend until the salsa is a smooth and loose consistency.

The salsa keeps well for up to 5 days in the fridge.

SALSA ROJA

RED SALSA

A salsa is the way we add heat to our dishes, so knowing how to make them fresh and from scratch is important to every Mexican. A *salsa roja* not only adds flavour, but it also adds a beautiful red colour to dishes. It can be made in advance and kept in the fridge for up to 5 days.

MAKES APPROX. 200ML

10 ARBOL CHILLIES, STEMS REMOVED
3 ROMA TOMATOES, HALVED
60G WHITE ONION, PEELED
1 LARGE GARLIC CLOVE, PEELED
1 TSP SEA SALT

Put the chillies, tomatoes, onion and garlic clove into a saucepan, add 450ml water and bring to the boil. Reduce the heat and simmer for 10 minutes until all the vegetables are soft.

Transfer the vegetables, tomatoes and chillies to a blender, reserving the water. Add 4 tablespoons of the reserved water and the salt. Blitz until smooth. If the salsa is too thick, add some more of the reserved water to adjust the consistency. Place in a bowl and serve. It keeps well in the fridge for up to 5 days.

ADEREZO DE CILANTRO

CORIANDER DRESSING

My dad used to make this dressing for us all the time. It reminds me of the type of dressing that you would find in a restaurant in Valle de Guadalupe, the wine region of Baja California, know for its fusion of Mexican and Mediterranean cuisine (page 90). At home, I make it every week, as it is very easy to whip up. I love pouring it onto everything: salads, roast baby potatoes, fried *taquitos*, tacos or roast vegetables!

MAKES APPROX. 250ML

40G FRESH CORIANDER, STALKS AND LEAVES, ROUGHLY CHOPPED
1 SMALL GARLIC CLOVE, ROUGHLY CHOPPED
1 MEDIUM EGG, AT ROOM TEMPERATURE
1 TSP WHITE WINE VINEGAR
½ TSP SEA SALT
150ML SUNFLOWER OIL

Put the coriander, garlic, egg, vinegar, salt and sunflower oil into a measuring jar.

Using a handheld blender, blitz the ingredients until you have a loose, smooth and creamy consistency. Using a hand blender helps to avoid the dressing splitting.

Put in a jar and store in the fridge for up to 2 days.

FINAL DULCE

SWEET ENDINGS

A good feast needs a good ending. In my family, there were plenty of feasts, especially at my grandma's house. As I've mentioned before, Mamá Mila was an excellent cook and she would always spoil us while we were visiting with the most delicious food and desserts. My favourite dessert was her pumpkin or sweet potato in syrup. I still remember the sweet aromas of *piloncillo* (raw sugar), cinnamon and spices coming out of her kitchen.

Mexico is a country with a sweet tooth and every region has its own preferred dessert. There are sweet food vendors that sell all sorts of delicious things, like *churros, nieve de garrafa* (artisanal ice cream), *pan dulce* (sweet bread) and many more. *Pan dulce* has hundreds of different varieties; a lot of them have funny and inventive names like: *piedra* (rock), *conchas* (shells), *niño envuelto* (wrapped up child) and *calvo* (bold). At home, my parents used to go to the *panaderia* (bakery) at least 4 times a week and would bring home a bag full of delicious *pan dulce*.

Mexicans love having something sweet, even after breakfast. Sometimes, we eat something sweet with a glass of milk or an *atole* (chocolate and corn hot beverage) for dinner. There are lots of tasty sweet things in the north and although I am just scratching the surface of all the incredible sweets we have, these are some of my favourites.

ARROZ CON LECHE

MEXICAN RICE PUDDING

Ⓥ

Rice pudding, although not originally from Mexico, is one of those desserts that has become very popular in our country. It can be eaten at any time of year; in winter, it is nice to eat it warm and, in the summer, it is perfect served cold with a sprinkle of cinnamon.

My mum makes an amazing rice pudding – her recipe has become quite popular among friends, so nowadays she gets asked to make it for events, birthday parties and gatherings. According to her, the secret of a good rice pudding is not to leave it unattended and constantly stir it to prevent sticking and burning.

SERVES 6

150G SHORT-GRAIN RICE

½ TSP SEA SALT

1 CINNAMON STICK

450ML WHOLE MILK

350ML CONDENSED MILK

50G *PILONCILLO* (RAW SUGAR) OR DEMERARA SUGAR

1 TSP VANILLA ESSENCE

GROUND CINNAMON, FOR DUSTING

Wash the rice and soak for 30 minutes, then drain.

Add the rice to a medium saucepan, together with 500ml water, salt and cinnamon stick. Bring to the boil over a medium heat. Reduce the heat and add the milk, condensed milk, sugar and vanilla essence.

Continue cooking the rice over a low heat, stirring from time to time to make sure that it does not stick to the bottom. This is the most important step because if it sticks, the rice will burn and it will change the flavour of the rice pudding.

After 25 minutes of cooking, the rice should be cooked through. Turn off the heat and let it cool slightly.

Serve in nice glasses, sprinkle over some ground cinnamon, then leave to set in the fridge or serve it at room temperature.

PASTEL DE DATIL

DATE LOAF CAKE

Ⓥ

Dates were introduced to the north of Mexico by the Spaniards that settled there in the sixteenth century. There are now more than a quarter of a million date palm trees in Baja California, with Mexicali and San Luis Río Colorado being the main date producers in Mexico. These little brown jewels are used in the preparation of sweets, desserts and some savoury dishes.

At home, I always make sure to have some in my cupboard, as they are good to use as a natural sweetener for smoothies. This is my favourite date recipe and my family seem to love it too, because every time I bake this cake, it's finished very quickly ...

SERVES 6

100G DATES, FINELY CHOPPED

75ML HOT WATER

130G UNSALTED BUTTER, SOFTENED

130G LIGHT BROWN SUGAR

2 EGGS, AT ROOM TEMPERATURE, BEATEN

200G SELF-RAISING FLOUR

½ TSP SEA SALT

1 TSP BAKING POWDER

50G WALNUTS, CHOPPED

VANILLA ICE CREAM OR WHIPPED CREAM, TO SERVE

Preheat the oven to 200°C (180°C fan/400°F/Gas 6). Line a 23 x 13cm non-stick loaf tin with baking parchment.

Soak 30g of the dates in the hot water for 10 minutes. Once soft, blend until smooth and set aside.

Cream the butter and sugar until fluffy and add the beaten eggs. Gently fold in the flour, salt and baking powder. Add the chopped dates, walnuts and the date water, folding in carefully.

Pour the mixture into the prepared tin and bake for around 40 minutes, or until cooked through. Check if it is cooked by inserting a skewer in the middle; if it comes out clean, it is cooked. Remove from the oven and leave to cool in the tin for 15 minutes, then transfer to a cooling rack.

Serve with some vanilla ice cream or whipped cream. Keep in an air-tight container for up to 3 days.

FLAN MEXICANO

MEXICAN FLAN

Ⓥ

This super creamy recipe for flan is easy to make and prepare a day in advance of being eaten. There are different recipes for making it; some add whole eggs (like this one), others only egg yolks, others with cream cheese. You can add an extra punch of flavour by including some grated orange zest on top, when serving.

In my family, my Auntie Laura makes the best recipe for flan. Hers is always smooth, light and creamy. This is the way I make it at home – I like to serve my flan with berries, but any seasonal fruit is fine.

SERVES 6–8

160G CASTER SUGAR

410ML CAN EVAPORATED MILK

397ML CAN CONDENSED MILK

120ML WHOLE MILK

4 EGGS

1 TBSP VANILLA ESSENCE OR ½ VANILLA POD

APPROX. 600ML WARM WATER, FOR WATER BATH (BAIN-MARIE)

Preheat the oven to 190°C (170°C fan/375°F/Gas 5). Grease and line a 21cm round tin, 5cm deep. Make sure this is the kind without a loose bottom, otherwise your flan mixture will leak.

Put the caster sugar into a medium saucepan with 2 tablespoons of water and melt over a medium–low heat, making sure it does not burn. Do not be tempted to stir the sugar with a spoon as this will make it crystallize.

Once the sugar becomes a caramel and is a dark golden-brown, transfer it quickly into the flan tin. Tip the tin in every direction to evenly spread the caramel in a coated layer before it sets. Place aside for the caramel to harden.

To make the custard, pour the evaporated milk, condensed milk, eggs and vanilla essence into a blender. Blend until all the ingredients are well combined.

Pour the custard into the tin; don't worry if you hear the caramel

cracking, this is normal. Cover the tin with foil and then place it in the middle of a large, deep oven tray. Pour warm water into the larger tray until it reaches halfway up the sides of the flan tin. Place the tray in the oven and bake for around 1 hour and 10 minutes.

Remove the flan from the oven and lift the foil to check if it is properly set by shaking the tin. It should wobble slightly. If it wobbles a lot, it needs to go back to the oven for a few more minutes.

Set aside to cool, then place it in the fridge until the next day.

To serve, run a sharp knife around the edge of the tin, then put a flat plate on top. In one swift, smooth movement, turn the tin upside down onto the plate and let the flan transfer, with the caramel juices following.

Serve with berries or enjoy by itself.

CAMOTES EN TACHA

SWEET POTATOES IN SYRUP

Ⓥ

Do you have a recipe that every time you make it, it transports you to a certain time in your life? I do, and this is the recipe that makes me think about my Mamá Mila in her kitchen in Culiacan, Sinaloa. She used to make this for me every time we spent Christmas with her. She would make a big jar just for me and we would travel back to Ensenada with it. I loved to eat it mixed with milk for supper.

The recipe, although originally from Puebla, a state in centre of the country, is nowadays made all around Mexico. It is called *en tacha*, because the pot used to make raw sugar out of the sugar cane is called a *tacha*.

Although Mamá Mila used to make this with pumpkin, this recipe can also be done with sweet potato, which I find is readily available throughout the year in supermarkets. The delicious spiced syrup takes the sweet potato to the next level.

SERVES 6–8

- 200G *PILONCILLO* (RAW SUGAR) OR DARK BROWN MUSCOVADO SUGAR
- 3 CLOVES
- 2 CINNAMON STICKS
- 4 SWEET POTATOES, PEELED AND CUT INTO THICK ROUND SLICES
- MILK, VANILLA ICE CREAM OR WHIPPED CREAM, TO SERVE

In a medium saucepan, put the *piloncillo* or sugar, cloves, cinnamon sticks and add 450ml water. Bring to the boil over a medium heat.

Once the *piloncillo* has melted, add the sliced sweet potato and reduce the heat. Cover with a lid and cook the sweet potatoes over a low heat for around 40 minutes. Don't stir as this will break the slices, just make sure that they don't burn.

When the water has become syrup, remove from the heat and leave to cool.

Serve with milk, vanilla ice cream or whipped cream.

This recipe can be made with pumpkin in place of the sweet potato. It can be stored in the fridge for up to 7 days.

CORICOS

MASA HARINA COOKIES

Coricos, also known as *tacuarines*, *coricoches* or *bizocochos*, are ring-shaped cookies made, usually, with corn flour. They are popular in the states of Sinaloa and Sonora, but are also found in the other northern states. These cookies became well known by the women who used to make them and sell them on the trains. There are different variations of it, a common variation is the *pinturitas* (little paints), made with the same dough, but the shape is different.

The original recipe is always made with corn flour, but these days, people mix wheat and corn flour, so that the cookies don't break easily. I like to stick to the traditional way; they have a stronger corn flavour and the smell takes me back to Culiacan, a city in Sinaloa, where I'd sit in my Mamá Mila's house, eating *coricos* with my siblings and cousins. My Auntie Esperanza always used to arrive to my grandma's house with a box of *coricos*; she is the expert in my family on making these delicious cookies.

At home in London, I make these for my children and love to get them involved. We'll make a few trays of coricos together and devour them in no time.

MAKES AROUND 30

- **70G *PILONCILLO* (RAW SUGAR) OR DARK MUSCOVADO SUGAR**
- **100G VEGETABLE SHORTENING**
- **40G BUTTER**
- **50G CASTER SUGAR**
- **1 LARGE EGG, AT ROOM TEMPERATURE**
- **250G MASA HARINA (GMO-FREE CORN FLOUR)**
- **¼ TSP SEA SALT**
- **1 TSP BAKING POWDER**

Start by making the *piloncillo* syrup. Add the *piloncillo* and 200ml water to a saucepan and simmer gently until the *piloncillo* has dissolved, the water has reduced by half and it looks like a syrup. Set aside to cool completely.

Cream together the vegetable shortening, butter and caster sugar. This can be done in a stand mixer with the paddle attachment. Add the egg and mix gently, followed by the masa harina, salt and baking powder. Continue mixing and add the *piloncillo* syrup.

Remove the dough from the mixer bowl and finish working it on the worktop. The dough needs to be moist, but not too wet that it sticks to your hands.

Once the dough is perfectly moist, separate the dough into 20g balls. Cover them with a tea towel to avoid them drying out.

Preheat the oven to 220°C (200°C fan/425°F/Gas 7) and line two baking trays with baking parchment.

To make a *corico*, grab a dough ball, by hand roll it into a 10cm thin rope and gently attach the ends to each other to form a circle. Place carefully onto a lined baking tray. Repeat with the remaining dough balls.

Bake for around 12 minutes until golden brown. Remove from the oven and leave to cool on the baking tray for 5 minutes before transferring to a cooling rack.

Enjoy with a nice cup of coffee or glass of cold milk.

COYOTAS

DULCE DE LECHE COOKIES

These delicious cookies are originally from the state of Sonora. According to 'Larousse Cocina', the Mexican gastronomic dictionary, the name *coyota* comes from the colour of the coyote as these cookies, when baked, are light brown. Another story, by *El Universal* newspaper, says that *coyota* is the name for the ladies who sold these cookies.

There are variations of *coyotas* fillings in different northern states, but what they all have in common is the *piloncillo* filling and the golden colour once they are baked. I love making them at home filled with a mixture of dulce de leche and walnuts.

MAKES 10

7G DRIED FAST-ACTION YEAST

150ML LUKEWARM WATER

50G CASTER SUGAR, PLUS 1 TSP

250G VEGETABLE SHORTENING

500G PLAIN FLOUR

¼ TSP SEA SALT

350G CAN CARAMEL

50G WALNUTS, FINELY CHOPPED

EQUIPMENT
TORTILLA PRESS OR ROLLING PIN
2 PIECES OF PLASTIC

Mix the yeast with the water and add 1 teaspoon of sugar to activate it. Let it double in size.

Meanwhile, cream the vegetable shortening using a stand mixer fitted with the paddle attachment, or by hand in a bowl for 3 minutes. Add the caster sugar and mix very well.

Next add the flour and salt and combine with the creamed shortening.

Then add the activated yeast and make sure that all the ingredients are properly combined to form a soft dough. Leave the dough to rest for 15 minutes.

Separate the dough into 45g balls.

Mix the caramel with the chopped walnuts and set aside, ready to fill the cookies.

Preheat the oven to 220°C (200°C fan/425°F/Gas 7) and line two baking sheets with baking parchment.

Use a tortilla press or rolling pin to form the cookies. Place a piece of plastic on the base of the tortilla press, put a dough ball in the middle, put the other piece of plastic on top and press, making a cookie 12cm diameter and 3mm thick. If using a rolling pin, place a piece of plastic on the worktop, put the dough ball in the middle, cover with the other piece of plastic and roll into a circle of the same size. Repeat with the remaining dough balls.

Place 1 tablespoon of the caramel and walnut mixture in the centre of one of the dough circles, put another circle on top and, using a fork, press the edges together. Use the same fork to make some holes in the centre, so the steam can escape and the cookies don't break. Repeat with the remaining dough circles and filling.

Place them carefully onto the lined baking trays and bake for 20 minutes. Remove from the oven and leave to cool on the trays for 5 minutes before transferring them onto a cooling rack.

Serve whilst still warm, so the centre is oozy.

OREJAS
PALMIERS
Ⓥ

Bread was introduced to Mexico by the Spanish, but it wasn't until the French intervention in the 1800s that the concept of *pan dulce* was born. The French introduced delicious pastries to Mexican cuisine and nowadays there are hundreds of different varieties, all with interesting names that usually refer to their shape; for instance *piedras* (rocks), *conchas* (shells) and *niño envuelto* (wrapped child).

Orejas, also known as Palmiers, are delicious, sweet, flaky cookies that are eaten as part of our breakfast or after dinner with a nice cup of coffee or milk.

MAKES 15

320G READY-ROLLED PUFF PASTRY SHEET
100G CASTER SUGAR
1 TSP GROUND CINNAMON

Preheat the oven to 220°C (200°C fan/425°F/Gas 7). Line a baking tray with baking parchment paper.

Roll out the puff pastry sheet on a clean worktop. Mix the sugar with the ground cinnamon.

Sprinkle some of the cinnamon sugar over the puff pastry and fold both ends inwards to meet in the middle. Repeat this process until you end up with a long pastry log. Make sure to sprinkle some of the cinnamon sugar in every fold.

Then, using a sharp knife, cut the pastry log into 1.5cm pieces. Lay the *orejas* cut-side up and, using a rolling pin, flatten them slightly. Add more cinnamon sugar and put them on the prepared baking tray.

Place the tray in the oven and bake for around 20 minutes, flipping them halfway through, so they bake evenly on both sides.

Remove from the oven and leave to cool for a few minutes on the baking tray, before transferring to a cooling rack.

Enjoy with a Coffee from the Pot (page 168).

CHIMANGOS

SUD BAJA CALIFORNIAN DOUGH PIECES

These delicious, deep-fried pieces of dough are a staple from Baja California Sur, eaten mostly in the evening with a cup of coffee or as a side with refried pinto beans with *queso fresco* (fresh cheese). They are not too sweet, so they go perfectly as an accompaniment for savoury dishes. Locals have been cooking these for generations, without many changes.

At home, I like to make these for my children when I'm feeling like I want to spoil them. Feel free to make them sweeter if you fancy by adding a bit more sugar.

SERVES 6

- 300G PLAIN FLOUR, PLUS 20G FOR DUSTING
- 1 TSP BAKING POWDER
- ½ TSP GROUND CINNAMON
- ½ TSP TABLE SALT
- 70G CASTER SUGAR
- 25G BUTTER, AT ROOM TEMPERATURE
- 1 MEDIUM EGG, AT ROOM TEMPERATURE
- 100ML WARM WATER
- 300ML VEGETABLE OIL

Place the flour in a large mixing bowl, add the baking powder, cinnamon, salt and sugar and mix well. Next add the butter and mix it into the flour using your fingertips until the flour looks like little breadcrumbs.

Whisk the egg and add to the flour, mixing well. Pour in the warm water and mix everything very well, until a soft and smooth dough forms. Remove it from the bowl and knead the dough for 5 minutes.

Put the dough back into the bowl, cover it with a clean tea towel and leave on the worktop away from the sun to rest for 10 minutes.

After the dough has rested, remove it from the bowl and, using a dough scraper, cut the dough into 4 equal pieces.

Heat the oil in a medium frying pan until it reaches 190°C (374°F).

Dust the worktop surface and the rolling pin with flour. Grab one of the dough pieces and roll it into a 4mm-thick rectangle. Cut them into your preferred shape with a knife – squares, triangles or rectangles are all fine.

Once the oil has reached the desired temperature, deep-fry the pieces of dough in small batches for about 2–4 minutes. Using a pair of tongs, turn them continuously to avoid burning. Remove the dough pieces from the oil when they look golden-brown in colour.

Enjoy with a cup of coffee or refried pinto beans and *queso fresco* or ricotta.

PALETAS DE MANGO, LIMÓN Y CHILE

MANGO, LIME & CHILLI ICE LOLLIES

Just like *aguas frescas* (page 170), *paletas* (ice lollies) are another Mexican staple. With dozens of flavour combinations, these refreshing street treats are easy to make at home. I remember my mum pouring this mango mixture into paper cups and then freezing them for us to enjoy, especially on a very hot day.

MAKES 10

3 PERFECTLY RIPE MANGOES
JUICE OF 1 LIME
4 TBSP AGAVE SYRUP
2 TBSP TAJIN OR CHILLI POWDER, MIXED WITH SALT

Peel the mangoes and, using a sharp knife, remove all the mango pulp, trying to cut very near to the pit.

Place the mango pulp, lime juice, agave syrup and 250ml water into a blender and blend until smooth.

Add some tajin chilli powder to each ice lolly container and pour in some of the mango mixture. Place an ice lolly stick into each mould and freeze until the following day.

To remove an ice lolly from the container, just place it under hot water for a few seconds and push it out of its case.

TAMALES DE PIÑA

PINEAPPLE TAMALES

Ⓥ

Tamales are steamed corn dough parcels of love. The origin of *tamales* in Mexico dates back to pre-Hispanic times. These have always been considered a celebration dish made for special occasions like local festivities, Christmas and birthday parties. Original *tamales* were a bit firmer, filled with vegetables that grew around the *milpa* (a piece of land designated to crop grow vegetables like maize, beans and courgettes). After the Spanish arrived in Mexico, the traditional recipe suffered many alterations, for instance, the use of pork lard and the introduction of meat fillings.

These days, the variation of *tamales* in Mexico is vast. Each region has its own way to make them, for example, in the south, they are made using banana leaves and in the north, we use dried corn husk leaves.

Sweet or savoury, *tamales* are eaten at any time of the day – for breakfast, lunch or dinner. They can be made at home or street bought. When Mexicans make *tamales* at home, we don't just make a few, we usually prepare enough to feed an army. The same rule applies for any dish that we consider special.

These pineapple *tamales* are one of our favourite sweet recipes. They are not difficult to make – just as long as you get the dough right, then you are onto a winner.

15 GOOD-SIZED DRIED CORN HUSK LEAVES, SPECIAL FOR TAMALES

200G UNSALTED BUTTER

60G CASTER SUGAR

300G MASA HARINA (GMO-FREE CORN FLOUR)

1 TSP BAKING POWDER

½ TSP SEA SALT

½ TSP GROUND CINNAMON

300ML PINEAPPLE JUICE

50ML PINEAPPLE SYRUP

1 TSP VANILLA ESSENCE

5 PINEAPPLE SLICES IN LIGHT SYRUP, FINELY CHOPPED

Place the corn husks in a large bowl and cover them with hot water to soften for around 15 minutes.

Meanwhile, cream the butter and caster sugar in a stand mixer, fitted with the paddle attachment, for 3 minutes.

Mix the masa harina with the baking powder, salt and cinnamon.

Keeping the mixer on, at low speed, add the masa harina mixture in small quantities, followed by the pineapple juice, syrup and vanilla. Continue mixing for 2 minutes.

Turn the mixer off, add the chopped pineapple and fold in with a spatula.

Remove the corn husk leaves from the water and drain to remove the excess.

Separate the dough into 80g balls, then spread the dough onto a corn husk, using either a spoon or your hands. Fold the husk or tie at both ends. Stack all the tamales into a steamer and steam for 1 hour.

Remove the steamer from the heat and leave to cool inside the pot for at least 20 minutes before eating. Remove the cooked tamal from the corn husk and discard the leaves before serving.

For a savoury tamal recipe, try the Sinaloa-style tamales on page 102.

PARA LA SED

FOR THE THIRST

In Mexico, it is custom to have a flavoured drink with every meal. For breakfast, a coffee and an orange juice are a must. For lunch, a refreshing *agua fresca* (flavoured water) made with fresh fruit is the perfect choice to wash things down. For dinner, something warm, like an *atole* (a corn-based drink) or a Mexican hot chocolate hits the spot.

Flavoured drinks are so popular that there are places that just sell these – like the *agua fresca* vendor or the *tamalero* who would sell *champurrado* (chocolate corn-based drink).

In this section, I gather some of my favourite drinks that I make at home. Some are classics to serve when gathering with friends, like the Frozen Margarita (page 164), others like the melon *Agua Fresca* (page 171) are drinks that I make on a regular basis to serve with a weekday meal.

FROZEN MARGARITA

Everyone loves a good margarita, and this is the cocktail I always make when I have friends round. Some people say it was created in Chihuahua, others that it is an American invention – but I like to believe those that say it was invented in my hometown of Ensenada, Baja California.

This version of the story says that it was created by a bartender at Hussong's Cantina, a bar widely considered an institution in the city. It has been there for more than 100 years with little change to the way it looks. It is an old canteen, with wooden floors and the same bartop since Hussong's opened its doors. Hussong's says their bartender made this famous drink, in honour of one of their customers named Margarita.

Whatever the origin of this delicious drink, it is now one of the most famous cocktails in the world. 100 per cent Mexican, 100 per cent *norte*. In the original recipe, the margarita glass is rimmed with fine salt, but I like to rim my glass with 'Tajín', a popular chilli powder, very well known among Mexicans.

MAKES 3

1 TBSP TABLE SALT OR TAJIN CHILLI POWDER TO RIM THE GLASSES
14 ICE CUBES
100ML LIME JUICE
100ML TEQUILA BLANCO
50ML AGAVE SYRUP
3 LIME WEDGES, TO DECORATE

Rim 3 margarita glasses with lime and dip in the salt or tajin chilli powder.

Combine the ice cubes, lime juice, tequila and agave syrup in a blender and blend until getting a slushy consistency.

Pour into the glasses and garnish with a lime wedge.

MICHELADA

TOMATO JUICE & BEER COCKTAIL

Why would you just drink an ordinary lager when you can have a *michelada*? This way to drink beer in Mexico is so popular that there is now a whole culture behind it. Just like the margarita, the creation of this concoction has several versions. I believe the story that says the *michelada* was created in San Luis Potosí in the 1970s. Tennis player Michel Esper used to order a lager with ice, lime and salt at his tennis club. The drink became popular among the club members, and they started to order a beer like Michel. Soon after, it was called *michelada*.

Nowadays, there are different ways to make a *michelada*. Some are a bit crazy, in my opinion, because they add too many ingredients – like prawns, chilli and sweets. I like to keep it simple, and this is my favourite way to enjoy a lager on a hot day.

MAKES 1

TAJIN CHILLI POWDER OR CHILLI POWDER AND SALT MIXED TOGETHER

50ML LIME JUICE

1 TBSP WORCESTERSHIRE SAUCE

6 DROPS OF TABASCO SAUCE

5 ICE CUBES

100ML CLAMATO OR TOMATO JUICE

330ML LAGER (I USE CORONA)

Rim a tall glass with the tajin chilli powder. Then add the lime juice, Worcestershire sauce, Tabasco sauce and combine. Pour in the Clamato juice, add the ice cubes and some of the lager.

Serve the *michelada* glass and remaining lager together. Top up the *michelada* glass with more lager as you wish.

PALOMA

GRAPEFRUIT & TEQUILA COCKTAIL

Someone said to me recently that a Paloma is the Mexican gin and tonic. I'm not sure if this is true but, in a similar vein, a Paloma is definitely a cocktail that I love to have on a hot, sunny day.

In Mexico, the recipe is very simple: Squirt soda (a grapefruit flavoured soda), blanco tequila, lime, ice and a salt-rimmed tall glass. The Paloma recipe below contains more ingredients, as it is difficult to find Squirt soda in the UK. I've replaced it with grapefruit juice, as I like the dusty pink hue that it gives to this cocktail. Like dusk, it's so beautiful.

MAKES 1

SALT, TO RIM THE GLASS

5 ICE CUBES, PLUS EXTRA FOR SHAKING IN THE COCKTAIL SHAKER

100ML GRAPEFRUIT JUICE

100ML INDIAN TONIC WATER

15ML LIME JUICE

50ML TEQUILA BLANCO

1 TBSP AGAVE SYRUP

1 SLICE OF GRAPEFRUIT, FOR DECORATION (OPTIONAL)

Rim the glass with salt and add the ice cubes.

In a cocktail shaker, add some ice and pour in the grapefruit juice, Indian tonic water, lime juice, tequila blanco and agave syrup. Shake to combine all the ingredients.

Pour the paloma mixture into the glass and garnish with a slice of grapefruit, if you like.

CHAMPURRADO

MASA HARINA HOT CHOCOLATE

Champurrado is one of the many *atole* varieties that we have in Mexico. An *atole* is a drink, usually made with corn and water. In pre-Hispanic times, these beverages were more than just a drink, they were considered a meal in itself, made of crushed corn tortillas and other masa-based ingredients, like beans. The word *atole* comes from the Nahuatl *atolli*, which means 'watered down'.

These days there are different types of *atoles* in Mexico, most of them are sweet and served as a drink. A *champurrado* is made with a base of corn dough and water, but milk and chocolate are added together with spices, like cinnamon. It is always served hot, ideal for a rainy, cold, winter day and it is the perfect companion for a *tamal*.

I love making *champurrado* during winter, to welcome my children when they arrive home from school.

MAKES 4 CUPS

- 40G MASA HARINA (GMO-FREE CORN FLOUR)
- 200ML WARM WATER
- 90G *PILONCILLO* (RAW SUGAR) OR DARK MUSCOVADO SUGAR
- 1 CINNAMON STICK
- 10G COCOA POWDER
- 450ML WHOLE MILK

In a bowl, mix the masa harina with the hot water, using a whisk to avoid the formation of lumps. Set aside.

Then, in a saucepan, add the dark muscovado sugar and cinnamon stick to 250ml water. Bring to the boil over a medium heat to dissolve the sugar. Reduce the heat and simmer for 3 minutes.

Add the cocoa powder and mix, followed by the milk.

When the mixture is hot, pour in the masa harina mixture. Using a whisk, mix well to avoid the mixture forming any lumps. Whisk until it comes to the boil, then let it simmer gently for 3 minutes. Turn off the heat and serve.

CAFÉ DE OLLA

COFFEE FROM THE POT

This interesting way of making coffee was my dad's favourite way to drink it. *Café de olla*, as its name says, is made in a clay pot and served in a clay cup. This technique started during the Mexican revolution among the soldiers. The coffee is brewed with spices, such as cinnamon, clove or star anise, with orange peel and sweetened with *piloncillo* (raw sugar).

Mexicans are big coffee drinkers and a morning cannot start properly without a good cup of invigorating coffee.

SERVES 3

- 4 TBSP *PILONCILLO* (RAW SUGAR) OR DARK MUSCOVADO SUGAR
- 1 CINNAMON STICK
- 4 TBSP GROUND COFFEE

Pour 660ml water into a saucepan, add the *piloncillo* or sugar and cinnamon stick. Bring to the boil over a medium heat.

Once the *piloncillo* or sugar has dissolved and the water is boiling, add the ground coffee and turn off the heat.

To serve, pass the coffee through a strainer.

TEJUINO

FERMENTED CORN DOUGH DRINK WITH SUGAR & LIME

A refreshing drink made with fermented corn dough, *piloncillo* (raw sugar), lime juice and salt, *Tejuino* is a drink native from Jalisco, a state in west Mexico, but also commonly made in a lot of the states of the north of Mexico. The corn dough is dissolved in hot water infused with *piloncillo* and lime juice is added. Then, this mix is left to ferment for two days. After two days, the solution looks like a jelly with a crust; this is mixed with water, ice, more lime juice and salt before being served in a glass with lots of ice.

There is another drink, also made with fermented corn in Chihuahua, that is called *tesgüino*. *Tesgüino* comes from the Nahuatl word *tecuin* meaning 'heart beating'. Although it also uses corn as the main ingredient, the process is more complex as the corn is left to ferment for a longer period of time in large clay pots specially crafted for this process. *Tesgüino* contains a small percentage of alcohol, formed during fermentation. For the Tarahumara people (an indigenous group in Chihuahua) and other ethnic groups (such as the Huichols), this drink is the drink of choice at their social events, religious and sports festivities. They also drink this during *tesgüinadas*, which are meetings in which important political and economic decisions are made.

SERVES AT LEAST 6

100G MASA HARINA (GMO-FREE CORN FLOUR)

100G *PILONCILLO* (RAW SUGAR) OR DARK MUSCOVADO SUGAR

1 LIME

TO SERVE
12 ICE CUBES
JUICE OF 3 LIMES
1 TSP SEA SALT

Make the corn dough by mixing the masa harina with 100ml water until a dough forms. Set aside.

In a saucepan, add 1 litre of water and dissolve the *piloncillo*. Bring to the boil over medium heat. Then add the corn dough in small quantities. Using a whisk, dissolve the dough in the sugar water. Whisk constantly to avoid the dough sticking to the bottom of the saucepan.

Cook for 5 minutes. Turn off the heat and squeeze in the lime juice. Cover with a tea towel and let the mixture ferment in a dark place for 2 days.

After 2 days, the mixture will look like jelly and will have a crust on the surface. This is now *tejuino*.

To serve the *tejuino*, pour half of the mixture into a blender with 1 litre water, and blend until it combines. Add the ice to a jug, pour the *tejuino* into it, along with the lime juice and salt. Mix well and serve in tall glasses.

AGUAS FRESCAS

This section wouldn't be complete without a good recipe for *agua fresca* (flavoured water). This is how we make the most out of a fruit by turning water into something exciting, refreshing and delicious. There are plenty of flavours for *agua fresca*, some of them have become classics; like hibiscus or *horchata*. Some states have a particular *agua fresca* that they drink during the hot months, for instance, in Chihuahua, they love *izquiate* (chia and lime) all year round. It is custom in households for meals to be served together with a refreshing *agua fresca*.

IZQUIATE

CHIA & LIME WATER

SERVES 4

2 TBSP CHIA SEEDS
JUICE OF 4 LIMES
100ML AGAVE SYRUP
ICE CUBES, TO SERVE

Place the chia seeds in 1 litre of water and leave to rehydrate for 30 minutes.

Add the lime juice, agave syrup and mix well. Serve with some ice.

AGUA FRESCA DE MANGO

MANGO WATER

SERVES 4

660ML MANGO PULP
JUICE OF 2 LIMES
100ML AGAVE OR SUGAR
   SYRUP
ICE CUBES
½ ALPHONSO MANGO,
   PEELED AND CUT INTO
   SMALL CUBES, TO GARNISH
   (OPTIONAL)

Pour 1 litre of water into a large pitcher, add the mango pulp, agave syrup and mix well.

Serve in glasses with some ice and some little pieces of mango.

AGUA FRESCA DE MELÓN

CANTALOUPE MELON WATER

SERVES 6

1 PERFECTLY RIPE CANTALOUPE MELON, PEELED, DESEEDED AND CUT INTO CHUNKS

100ML AGAVE OR SUGAR SYRUP

ICE CUBES

100G CANTALOUPE MELON, PEELED, CUT INTO 1CM CUBES TO GARNISH (OPTIONAL)

Pour 1 litre of water into a blender, add the pieces of cantaloupe melon and agave syrup. Blend until smooth.

Once blended, pour it into a pitcher. Add ice and the little pieces of fresh melon. Serve in glasses.

AGUA FRESCA DE PEPINO

CUCUMBER & LIME WATER

SERVES 6

2 CUCUMBERS, PEELED, DESEEDED AND CUT IN CHUNKS

JUICE OF 3 LIMES

150ML AGAVE OR SUGAR SYRUP, PLUS EXTRA IF NEEDED

ICE CUBES

THINLY SLICED CUCUMBER AND LIME, TO GARNISH (OPTIONAL)

Pour 1 litre of water into a blender, add the pieces of cucumber, lime juice and agave syrup. Blend until smooth.

Once blended, pour it into a pitcher. Add ice and the little pieces of fresh cucumber. Serve in glasses.

MEXICAN MENUS

QUICK WEEKNIGHT DINNERS

These dishes are for those evenings that you are short of time, but still want to eat something delicious. They can be made in no time at all – an easy win on nights like these is to use shop-bought tortillas and frozen mango.

MENU 1

PRAWN & CHEESE TACOS (PAGE 64)
SPRING RICE (PAGE 55)
GUACAMOLE (PAGE 27)
MANGO WATER (PAGE 170)

MENU 2 Ⓥ

POTATO FRIED TAQUITOS (PAGE 42)
COURGETTES WITH SWEETCORN (PAGE 50)
GREEN RICE (PAGE 57)
MANGO WATER (PAGE 170)

FOR A COLD WINTER'S DAY

These two menus are perfect for cold, rainy days. All the dishes are just what you need when the weather is miserable and you need to stay indoors.

MENU 1

SINALOA-STYLE LAMB BARBACOA (PAGE 98)
PINTO BEANS FROM THE POT (PAGE 22)
RED RICE (PAGE 56)
CREAMY RED SALSA (PAGE 144)
FLOUR TORTILLAS (PAGE 16)
PALMIERS (PAGE 156)
MASA HARINA HOT CHOCOLATE (PAGE 168)

MENU 2 Ⓥ

CHEESE BROTH (PAGE 48)
NORTHERN-STYLE WHITE CABBAGE (PAGE 51)
RED RICE (PAGE 56)
GUACAMOLE (PAGE 27)
FLOUR TORTILLAS (PAGE 16) Ⓥⓞ
MEXICAN RICE PUDDING (PAGE 148)
MASA HARINA HOT CHOCOLATE (PAGE 168)

FOR A SUMMER'S DAY

Summer is my favourite time of the year. I spent a lot of my childhood outdoors as the weather in Ensenada was always nice. My parents were amazing at hosting gatherings during the summer months, so I hope these two menus inspire you to similarly cook more Northern-style barbecues at home.

MENU 1

SINALOA-STYLE GRILLED CHICKEN (PAGE 125)
GREEN AGUACHILE (PAGE 81)
GREEN RICE (PAGE 57)
TOMATO, ONION & JALAPEÑO SALSA (PAGE 28)
PINEAPPLE TAMALES (PAGE 160)
PALOMAS (PAGE 167)

MENU 2

BAJA FISH OR CAULIFLOWER TACOS (PAGE 62)
PRAWN CEVICHE TOSTADAS (PAGE 66)
WATERCRESS SALAD (PAGE 53)
GUACAMOLE (PAGE 27)
MANGO, LIME & CHILLI ICE LOLLIES (PAGE 159)
CANTALOUPE MELON WATER (PAGE 171)

FOR TWO

These recipes are perfect to make on a smaller scale, without compromising flavour. I love to make these dishes for my husband and I, on those days when our children have arranged things to do with friends.

MENU 1

PORK IN A RED CHILLI SAUCE (PAGE 114)
JUST-FRIED PINTO BEANS (PAGE 45)
RED RICE (PAGE 56)
FLOUR TORTILLAS (PAGE 16)
MICHELADAS (PAGE 166)

MENU 2

SKATE WING SOUP (PAGE 84)
GUACAMOLE (PAGE 27)
TORTILLA CHIPS
JUST-FRIED PINTO BEANS (PAGE 45)
CUCUMBER & LIME WATER (PAGE 171)

FOR A CROWD

This is crowd-pleasing food perfect for those occasions when you have a full house to impress. These are dishes that are great to prep in advance, make big batches of and feed many mouths.

MENU 1

BEEF BIRRIA (PAGE 96)
CORN TORTILLAS (PAGE 18)
OIL-BASED SALSA (PAGE 140)
SWEET POTATOES IN SYRUP (PAGE 152)
FROZEN MARGARITAS (PAGE 164)

MENU 2 ⓥ

TOMATO ENCHILADAS WITH CHEESE
(PAGE 46)
GUACAMOLE (PAGE 27)
JUST-FRIED PINTO BEANS (PAGE 45)
DULCE DE LECHE COOKIES (PAGE 155)
MICHELADAS (PAGE 166)

FOR A LAZY WEEKEND BRUNCH

For those weekends when you have more time to enjoy the cooking
process and are seeking something cosy and comforting to eat.

MENU 1

DRIED SHREDDED BEEF WITH POTATOES
(PAGE 109)
JUST-FRIED PINTO BEANS (PAGE 45)
RED RICE (PAGE 56)
CORN TORTILLAS (PAGE 18)
CHIMANGOS (PAGE 158)
FROZEN MARGARITAS (PAGE 164)

MENU 2 Ⓥ

MEXICAN HOT DOGS (PAGE 116) Ⓥ𝗈
NACHOS (PAGE 127) Ⓥ𝗈
TOMATO, ONION & JALAPEÑO SALSA
(PAGE 28)
GUACAMOLE (PAGE 27)
MICHELADAS (PAGE 166)

FOR VEGETARIANS

MENU 1 Ⓥ

STUFFED LONG GREEN PEPPERS (PAGE 40)
WHITE RICE WITH SWEETCORN (PAGE 57)
CAESAR SALAD (PAGE 54)
GUACAMOLE (PAGE 27)
MASA HARINA COOKIES (PAGE 154)

MENU 2 Ⓥ

COURGETTES WITH CHEESE (PAGE 50)
GREEN RICE (PAGE 57)
CORIANDER DRESSING (PAGE 145)
DULCE DE LECHE COOKIES (PAGE 155)
CANTALOUPE MELON WATER (PAGE 171)

FOR A CELEBRATION

There's no better way to celebrate a birthday or good news than sharing good company and good food. Why not treat them to a Mexican feast?

MENU 1

ASADA TACOS (PAGE 20)
CORN TORTILLAS (PAGE 18)
FLOUR TORTILLAS (PAGE 16)
TOMATO, ONION & JALAPEÑO SALSA (PAGE 28)
GUACAMOLE (PAGE 27)
CREAMY RED SALSA (PAGE 144)
PINTO BEANS FROM THE POT (PAGE 22)
CHARRED CHILLIES AND SPRING ONIONS IN A
SOY & LIME MARINADE (PAGE 31)
WATERMELON WEDGES WITH LIME
AND CHILLI POWDER
CUCUMBER & LIME WATER (PAGE 171)

MENU 2 Ⓥ

SINALOA-STYLE TAMALES (PAGE 102) Ⓥⓔ
JUST-FRIED PINTO BEANS (PAGE 45)
RED RICE (PAGE 56)
PARTY PASTA SALAD (PAGE 38)
MEXICAN FLAN (PAGE 150)
FROZEN MARGARITAS (PAGE 164)

THE NORTHERN BORDER: A SYMBIOTIC RELATIONSHIP BETWEEN TWO NATIONS

Mexico is a big country, but it used to be even bigger, also comprising the southern states of the USA: California, Nevada, Texas, Utah, New Mexico, Arizona, Colorado and some parts of Oklahoma, Kansas and Wyoming. In February 1848, Mexico ceded 55 per cent of its territory to the United States, signing the Treaty of Guadalupe Hidalgo and ending the ongoing war between the two countries.

As part of the terms of the treaty, the US paid Mexico $6 million and promised to recognize all Mexicans living in the ceded states as American citizens. Some Mexicans decided to repatriate and return to Mexico, but those who stayed became second-class citizens, suffering at the hands of the Americans who had settled in those regions. Despite this, the Mexicans who stayed kept up their traditions, continuing to cook their family recipes and giving birth to what we now know as TexMex food.

The influence between the two nations flows both ways. Northerners have adopted some of the American classics and given them a Mexican touch. For instance, American hot dogs are as popular as *tacos*, but we add a lot of Mexican toppings, like pickled jalapeños, *salsa bandera* and chorizo (page 116). We go crazy for burgers, which we also have a Mexican version of. We also enjoy those massive, thick burritos, but we call them *percherones*.

The relationship between the two nations is constantly evolving. Life in the border cities changes every day, getting more complex in recent years. Because of political instability in Latin America, people travel north in hope of new beginnings and a better life.

INDEX

A NORTH MEXICAN PANTRY

There are some essential ingredients that are important to stock in your pantry to cook Mexican food. Most of these ingredients have a long shelf life and are sold in small portions, so you don't end up using a little and storing a lot. I hope you will learn to love them and use them widely in your cooking. These days, it is much easier to find authentic ingredients than it was 20 years ago, when I first arrived in London.

ESSENTIALS
Good red tomatoes are essential in a Mexican kitchen, as well as white onions, garlic, avocados, limes and fresh coriander. I make sure that I always have these fresh ingredients in, as well as the basic store cupboard spices: cinnamon, clove, cumin, oregano, and marjoram.

CHILLIES
A lot of Mexican recipes call for dried or fresh chillies, depending on whether they're adding heat or flavour. In my pantry I'm always fully stocked on chillies, especially dried ones that last for a long time. My favourite dried chillies are: *guajillo*, *ancho*, *arbol*, *pasilla*, *morita*, New Mexico and *chiltepin*. These last two are difficult to find in the UK, but you can replace them for *piquín* chillies, which are widely available online.

The Anaheim green pepper is a fresh chilli used in a lot of northern recipes, but a great alternative is the Turkish long green pepper, 'Yesil Tatli Biber', easily found in Turkish grocery shops. It gives the same aromatic flavour to broths, soups or stews.

FLOUR
To make good wheat or corn tortillas, you really need to buy good flour. I like buying organic wheat flour for when I make northern-style flour tortillas (page 16) – I use Doves Farm. For the corn tortillas (page 18), any GMO-free flour is perfect.

CHEESE
Trying to find Mexican cheeses in the UK is almost impossible, but there are great alternatives. Feta or Greek Manouri are the perfect replacements to *queso fresco*. Wensleydale can be used instead of *cotija*. A combination of Cheddar and mozzarella cheeses works to replace the *chihuahua* cheese used in *quesadillas* or stuffed peppers. Turkish or Persian grocery shops are a good place to find these alternatives.

JARS AND CONDIMENTS
Some of our northern Mexican recipes wouldn't be the same without the addition of the umami flavour, and we achieve this by using unusual ingredients that you wouldn't typically relate with Mexican cuisine, like Maggi sauce, soy sauce, Worcestershire sauce and Clamato. If you can't find Clamato, which is a combination of clam and tomato juice, then any spiced tomato juice or Bloody Mary mix works well.

ONLINE RESOURCES
When it comes to speciality ingredients, there are plenty of places to buy them online.

Cool Chile Co [www.coolchile.co.uk]: for fresh tomatillos, *totopos*, *poblano* peppers and jalapeños.

MexGrocer [www.mexgrocer.co.uk]: for dried chillies, good GMO-free nixtamalized corn flour and spicy salsas.

Mextrade [www.mextrade.co.uk]: for excellent ready-prepared corn tortillas, if you don't have time to make your own.

Mexican Mama [www.mexican-mama.com]: a reliable source for good store cupboard ingredients, like good quality nixtamalized corn flour.

ACKNOWLEDGEMENTS

I dedicate this book to my parents. To my dad – my beloved *apa* – Martin Pinedo Sanchez, who was the force of our north Mexican kitchen. The one who would wake up very early to make breakfast and freshly made flour tortillas. We were so lucky to have you as our dad. I will be forever grateful for all the cooking lessons you gave me and within these pages lays the result of them. I hope I have made you proud. I'm sure you're still making *carne asada* in heaven. To my *mami*, Nery, for teaching me all her family recipes, tips and secrets. Thank you for always being there to support me and for your unconditional love. Your food has always been delicious.

Thank you to my sister, Cynthia, who helped me choose the recipes for the book and listened to me hundreds of times – even when I called her late at night. To the rest of my big family in Ensenada and Sinaloa, who have followed my cooking journey closely. I'm sure our Mamà Mila is very happy wherever she is.

A very special thanks to my wonderful little family; my husband, Russell, and my lovely children, Miah and Emilio. Thanks a million for being so patient and supportive – this book is yours as much as it is mine. Thank you for eating all the Mexican food that I recipe-tested for months. I will cherish all the moments that we talked about this cookbook, especially with El Marido, who doesn't cook but contributed great ideas. You three are my everything and I love you very much – to infinity and beyond.

This book wouldn't have happened without the great support of the amazing team at Pavilion and HarperCollins. Lucy Smith, who was the one that got in touch with me – who loved, listened and believed in my idea of writing a book about the north of Mexico. Special thanks to my wonderful editor, Ellen Simmons, for being so patient and replying to all my emails guiding me through the process of writing my first cookbook. Also, thank you to Stephanie Milner for believing in my book and helping making *sopes* during the photoshoot. Thanks to the incredible designer Laura Russell, for such beautiful design.

A big thanks to the super team behind the photoshoot: Joe Woodhouse, Esther Clark, Florence Blair and Caitlin MacDonald. I had so much fun cooking, eating and taking pictures of the book with you. It was a lot of work but it went so quickly – I totally enjoyed every single minute of it. What a great experience!

Thank you to all my friends who tested my recipes: Emily, Olia, Fabi, Claudia, Manuel and Ariane – I love cooking for and with you. Thank you for making me believe in myself and stop suffering so much from impostor syndrome. You guys are my biggest fans and I love you very much.

Writing this cookbook is a dream that I never thought would become a reality. It is the culmination of many years of hard work and overcoming self-doubt. I am immensely grateful to all the people that I have met during this incredible cooking journey; this book is for you and all those who have followed my Mexican Food Memories blog.

And lastly, but most importantly, to the incredible people from the north of Mexico who have a heart as big as the entire country. Thank you for being the inspiration for this book.

Pavilion
An imprint of HarperCollins*Publishers* Ltd
1 London Bridge Street
London SE1 9GF

www.harpercollins.co.uk

HarperCollins*Publishers*
1st Floor, Watermarque Building
Ringsend Road Dublin 4
Ireland

10 9 8 7 6 5 4 3 2 1

First published in Great Britain by
Pavilion, an imprint of HarperCollins*Publishers* Ltd 2024

ISBN 978-0-00-859948-5

This book contains FSC™ certified paper and other controlled
sources to ensure responsible forest management.

For more information visit:
www.harpercollins.co.uk/green

Printed and bound in Malaysia by Papercraft

Publishing Director: Stephanie Milner
Design Director: Laura Russell
Editor: Ellen Simmons
Designer: James Boast
Photography: Joe Woodhouse
Food stylist: Esther Clark
Food assistant: Caitlin MacDonald
Prop stylist: Florence Blair
Illustrator: Jessica Benhar
Copy editor: Vicky Orchard
Proofreader: Kate Reeves-Brown
Indexer: Ruth Ellis
Production controller: Grace O'Byrne

WHEN USING KITCHEN APPLIANCES PLEASE ALWAYS FOLLOW
THE MANUFACTURER'S INSTRUCTIONS